PRESENTED TO

_____

FROM

_____

DATE

_____

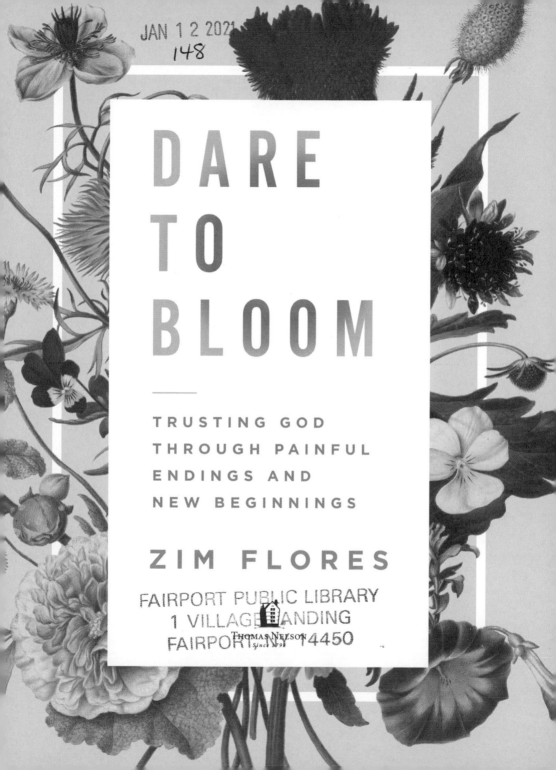

DARE TO BLOOM

TRUSTING GOD
THROUGH PAINFUL
ENDINGS AND
NEW BEGINNINGS

ZIM FLORES

THOMAS NELSON
Since 1798

Published in Nashville, Tennessee, by Thomas Nelson. Thomas Nelson is a registered trademark of HarperCollins Christian Publishing, Inc.

Thomas Nelson titles may be purchased in bulk for educational, business, fund-raising, or sales promotional use. For information, please email SpecialMarkets@ThomasNelson.com.

Art direction and interior design: Tiffany Forrester

Interior layout: Mallory Collins

ISBN: 978-1-4402-1863-9 (Audiobook)
ISBN: 978-1-4402-1865-3 (eBook)
ISBN: 978-1-4002-1869-1 (Hardcover)

Printed in China

20 21 22 23 24 GRI 10 9 8 7 6 5 4 3 2 1

To my Lord. You are my hope for today and the only Hero of my tomorrows. All that is good in me comes from You.

To my mom. My first example. Your story is a bold testament to God's relentless grace. I will forever be your Adaugo. A huru m gi n'anya.

To my husband. Thank you for cherishing, believing in, and loving me through each new beginning.

To you. May the discomfort of the unfamiliar always remind you to whom you belong.

CONTENTS

INTRODUCTION

GOD KNEW THE EXACT MOMENT your eyes would trace the lines of this page. He understood the depths of your circumstance before you ever picked up this book. He balanced His weighty promises over the scale of your life when you cried out for help. You are blooming, even now.

And if you're anything like me, you probably didn't get it right on the first try. Perhaps you thought that a life in full bloom would be one without pain. But growth demands it. Maybe you thought you'd be a little further along. Or a lot richer. Or much more successful. But God has you right where He wants you.

Over the course of our lives, we'll find ourselves in different seasons. Seasons of hardships, seasons of abundance, seasons of seeking, seasons of struggle. Each has an ordained purpose. As you read about my journey in the following pages, I encourage you to pay close attention to how God is calling you to grow and bloom in your own, distinct way.

> If there's one thing I've done a lot of in life, it's starting over.

In daring to bloom over and over throughout the years, I've discovered dozens of new identities along the way. I've called myself many things, pegging my worth to where I lived, whom I knew, and what job I had. And with every shifting season, I struggled to identify the new person I was becoming. At times, it felt like being caught in an undercurrent, not knowing which direction was up or down.

It's a tricky concept, identity. And it's one that's made even more difficult when the things we hold as truth change right before our eyes. If there's one thing I've done a lot of in life, it's starting over.

Beginning again.

Embracing radical change.

Trusting God through painful endings and new beginnings.

My story doesn't start with me—no one's story does. My story begins with my grandmother, who lost her husband during the Biafran War in Nigeria. She was left to raise five children on her own. It was a brand-new beginning for her. Overnight, she went from being a loving wife to a widow. And my mom and her siblings went from living in the security of a two-parent home to surviving on one income.

My mother grew up in a small, two-bedroom home in Nigeria with her four siblings. She graduated high school and entered college. Eventually it was recommended for her to marry my father—a common practice in those days. And then eventually

after that, she moved from sunny village life in Eastern Nigeria to the brute cold of Mankato, Minnesota, where she knew no other soul but her husband's.

A new beginning.

She would learn in that season how to be a young wife and how to fend for herself, far away from everything that she knew. She gave birth to me in a hospital in 1988, entangled within a web of her own thoughts, and completely alone.

When I was just a few years old, a tragedy happened in our little family that would forever shape the rest of our lives. One night, my mother stumbled upon my father's hidden gun. Trapped in a marriage that was physically, emotionally, financially, and mentally abusive, she began to plan her escape, which would include my brother and me. By the time my father came back from his next business trip, we were gone.

Though my first cross-country road trip was laced with uncertainty, it was the beginning of my love for exploration. We were a young family trying to hold firm to the promise of reinvention. My father eventually left the country for a new life in Nigeria, and we found hope in the safety of a small women's shelter. We were starting over.

My early childhood was composed of a lot of dissonance, estranged chords, and sustained melodies, until we finally ended up where it all started: Rochester, Minnesota.

Another new beginning.

My childhood was full of adventure. Back in those days, roaming the streets freely was a common respite for my brother and me. As a nurse my mom worked twelve-hour shifts, getting us dressed before school and then preparing breakfast for us before she left for her shift at the hospital. Since we lived in an apartment complex only a block away from our school, we woke up, got dressed, grabbed our premade breakfast, and walked over to our elementary school.

I had spent my entire young life as an outlier.

A few years later, when I was eight years old, my mom accepted a position at one of the leading hospitals in North Carolina. We made a move from the familiar to the unfamiliar, just like my mother and grandmother had done many years before. I had spent my entire young life as an

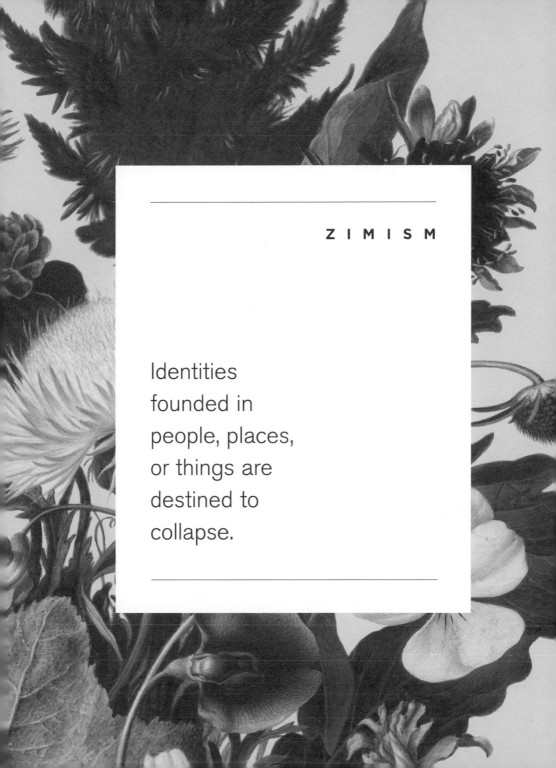

ZIMISM

Identities
founded in
people, places,
or things are
destined to
collapse.

outlier, accepted by a community who didn't look like me. In Minnesota, many were curious about my given name: Zimuzor Ugochukwu—Zim for short. My friendships were strengthened in my difference.

Although North Carolina was another new beginning—an opportunity for a fresh start—I hated it. I had new challenges to contend with. In addition to leaving my old friends behind, I went from being an outlier in a white community where I *was* accepted, to being an outlier in a new, mostly Black community in North Carolina where I *wasn't* accepted. I was ridiculed and mocked. No one wanted to be my friend. I heard the sneers as I passed by other kids. This was the first time in my life that I denied my identity, trying to convince myself and others that I wasn't African. Attempting to blend in eventually led to experimenting with theft.

My time growing up was spent wrestling between these two worlds. In one circle I was accepted; in the other, rejected. At the root of it, though, I didn't understand my true identity. Who I thought I was shifted with each circumstance. Every time I was rejected, I felt completely worthless, often pretending to be someone else.

ZIMISM

I no longer
wanted to be
the travel girl.
I wanted to
be God's girl.

At an early age, I had to become comfortable with being different because there was nobody who looked like me. I was used to being unconventional, and new beginnings felt like home. Toward the end of high school, I fared a little better. I began to embrace all of the weird, quirky things about me. I became transient, able to move freely among different social circles. I found my confidence in my ability to speak to different types of people and found my brand of cool in that way. I wasn't popular, but people knew me. I talked to the jocks, the nerds, and everybody in between. And it was during this period of my life that I began to feel equipped. As I clung to my new identity, I carried it like a banner of truth.

> I had to become comfortable with being different.

148

I went off to college, and I dabbled in a few unconventional things. When I was nineteen years old, I cloned a gene that had similarities to a genetic disorder (I'm a biologist by trade). And I was the youngest appointed precinct judge for the state of North Carolina. Among other things, it was during this time in college that I cut my teeth in organizing communities both on and off-line. I started an organization to help open up an international civil rights museum, and with my best friend, we ran an anti-tobacco organization, being the youngest in the nation to do so.

Following a vigorous application process, I was selected for the prestigious Henry Luce Fellowship. I sold everything I owned and moved to India. New country, new language, new culture, and a new identity. After a transformative year abroad, I ended up back in California with my mom, having spent every dollar that I earned on travel. I was peppered with questions like: *Are you still going to apply for medical school? When are you planning to enroll in nursing school? How about starting with your post-doc?*

It was during this time that I very bravely told my mom that I was going to try something new. I had a few hundred dollars in my bank account and bought a Greyhound bus ticket to San Francisco, where I lived on a couch for six months and held down four jobs. I worked as a nanny, sold luxury sunglasses, helped a friend start her company, and worked at a tech startup. At the time it would have been easy for me to pin my identity to my circumstances and the jobs I was holding.

Then in 2013 I started my first company, Travel Noire, helping Black millennials travel with deeper meaning. We were a travel media company that hosted small-group experiences around the world: sixty trips per year across five different continents. Business was booming. We earned seven figures in revenue every single year. As a tiny team of four, we were named by Fast Company as one of the most innovative companies in the world. I became a Forbes "30 Under 30" entrepreneur. By mid-2017, we were serving about two million travelers—every single month.

ZIMISM

We are all in
a perpetual
cycle of new
beginnings.

And then one day I felt the Lord leading me to give it all up. There I was, with my identity so intertwined with what I created that I had forgotten my Creator. Everything that I had worked so hard for, I sacrificed for a greater promise and a new identity—once and for all.

A divine encounter with God led me to create the *Bloom Podcast*. *Bloom* is a column-style podcast, applicable to each season of a woman's journey. It defines what it means to live passionately for God in a lukewarm world. It encourages us to embrace every season that we're called to. From dating and purpose to identity and sacrifice, *Bloom* covers the areas of a woman's journey that matter most. I've had the honor of receiving letters from women around the country— expressions of profound vulnerability and seeking during their times of struggle and transition—and I've used this forum as a way to share hope and healing, not just for those who write in but for anyone listening.

> We were serving about two million travelers—every single month.

Dare to Bloom is, in essence, a book about navigating new beginnings. By choice or by circumstance, we all find ourselves in seasons where we have to start over. Seasons where we have to transition. And it's easy to forget who we are in these times. Our identities are often bound to our conditions, but in those moments, where do we look to find our hope? Our identities never belong in our status, our relationships, our financial situations, our careers, or our hometowns. Our identities belong to God and God alone.

Dare to Bloom is about re-creating our identity in God. It's about learning to trust the process of transitioning. It's about abandoning who society tells us we are based on what we're going through. We spend so much of our lives affixing ourselves to our circumstance that we miss out on the freedom of who God says we are. Discovering our identity comes first with uprooting everything we've ever known about who we are.

As Christians, we are taught that our identity is found in Christ alone, but if we're honest with ourselves, we often find our self-worth in anything but Christ. We believe we are only as good as our last success. I had to learn again and again that this isn't true, with each of the many times in my life when I've had to start over.

I started over when I sold everything I owned and moved to India.

I started over with three hundred dollars in my bank account when I packed up and left for San Francisco.

I started over when, knowing only one person, I moved to Chicago.

I started over when I sold my company.

And countless other times, I started over.

> We believe we are only as good as our last success.

Embracing our identity and starting over means packing light. Many times we want to bring all of our comforts from previous seasons into the new season. But God may want us to bring nothing. In this way, we won't simply start over; we'll thrive. Thriving during a transition means discovering our every-season purpose.

In the Bible, Jeremiah was given an assignment by God: to pluck up and to break down. To destroy and to overthrow. To build and to plant. He was given an every-season purpose that he could never have accomplished if his identity had been rooted in each of those things. His firm foundation in God meant that he could weather the criticism when he was destroying or breaking down, and that he could manage the praise when he was building up and planting.

Dare to Bloom matters because people's tides are turning more than ever now. People are experiencing transitions now. They are starting over right now. And some people are losing themselves in the process. This was a hard lesson that I had to learn, and it's a hard lesson that you also may be learning. This book answers this question: *Who are you when the thing you've identified yourself with is no longer there?*

I'm writing *Dare to Bloom* because with each turn of a new season, each time I started over, this is the book that I so desperately needed. By choice or by circumstance, we will each encounter new beginnings. We'll find ourselves in new surroundings, and more often than not, we'll lose sight of who we *thought* we were.

When our identities are bound to our circumstances, it's easy to lose hope when things change. But hopefully, with time, we'll eventually learn that our identity doesn't come from our status, our relationships, our careers, or our hometowns; it belongs to God, and God alone. This book will challenge you to look past the fleeting security found in people, things, and circumstances and become laser-focused about your identity in Christ.

Even as our identities are challenged day by day, we can find confidence to reclaim our identity in God, who is unchanging through it all. In these chapters, it is my prayer that you find the courage to reclaim who you really are, edge closer to your ultimate purpose, and eagerly participate in your own story—even though you may not know the outcome. Navigating seasons of transitions can be tough, but I hope that as you turn each page, you find fresh wisdom when you feel stuck and inspiration to follow God into the unknown.

> When our identities are bound to our circumstances, it's easy to lose hope when things change.

In this book, I share stories of surprising life shifts, tragedies, and new beginnings, and how each helped uncover a new layer of my identity. You'll also hear about the struggles I still have—despite having started over so many times—with affixing my identity to the One who matters most. It's important for me to share my life (and my mistakes) with you because I deeply believe my story creates tension, and that God alone provides the resolve.

To some, I may look like I have it all together: I sold my first company in my twenties, I've won many awards for my work, I own several brands, and I travel the world. But it's the furthest thing from the truth. For so long, my identity existed in the silo of my own work and success; when my success was stripped from me, I felt broken beyond recognition.

I like to use the subject of travel as a conduit for many of my life lessons because through it I'm confronted with my own personal flaws. And those flaws can only be reconciled and transformed in the hands of the Father. I have been blessed to have built a business that allowed me to travel, and even after giving it up, I still have the freedom to work from anywhere in the world. I recognize that to travel as frequently as I do is a privilege, which I do not take for granted. My heart is not to boast, but my hope is to share how God has used even the simplest of occurrences to transform and renew my mind.

I deeply believe my story creates tension, and that God alone provides the resolve.

Throughout I've shared images from my travels, allowing you to look through my lens of the world for brief moments.

As you read this book, I invite you to be vulnerable and honest with yourself. Allow yourself to be broken so that God can do the necessary work of knitting your identity together with His. *Dare to Bloom* isn't just a phrase as much as it is a way of life. The ethos comes from the perseverance to do all that God has called us to do, despite what the enemy or society has to say about who we are. No matter your circumstance, you belong to God. He is desperate for you and holds your past, present, and future identity in His hand.

Bloom on.

Throughout I've shared images from my travels, allowing you to look through my lens of the world for brief moments.

1

AN
ALL-WEATHER
PURPOSE

WHAT IF I TOLD YOU THAT GOD has a purpose for every single season of your life? Purpose doesn't end once we find it; rather, purpose is something that continues to unfold and evolve throughout our lives.

Each season—fall, winter, spring, and summer—has its own place and purpose in nature. Plants that bloom in some seasons die in others. Our favorite seasons are often dictated by personal milestones—the hobbies, holidays, or even birthdays that fall within them. Even still, one thing is for certain: the seasons are fixed. When one season ends, another begins. In the same way, each season in our life will have its own place and purpose; the more we're able to identify that purpose, the better equipped and in tune we will be to God's Will for our life.

Purpose has become a popular topic these days, and finding one's purpose has become such an obsession that there are hundreds of resources to help us discover it. When people reference purpose, it tends to center on what I like to call the all-weather purpose—or the every-season purpose—one that is large and meaningful and spans a lifetime. Sometimes we spend a lifetime trying to uncover it. We read books about it. We dream about it. We create vision boards for it. We even pray about it.

> "See, I have set you this day over nations and over kingdoms, to pluck up and to break down, to destroy and to overthrow, to build and to plant."
>
> **JEREMIAH 1:10**

For some, with ample time spent with God, we uncover it. But for many others a sense of purpose completely eludes them forever.

A lesser known, equally powerful concept is one that uncovers a purpose in each new chapter of life—also known as our seasonal purpose. This type of purpose is specific to a finite period of time that may span a few weeks, a few months, or a few years.

Our ultimate purpose—what God has placed us on this earth to accomplish—cannot be found apart from Him. We can read all the books on purposes. We can journal from morning to evening. We can take courses and talk to counselors. But God's purpose for us can only be uncovered in Him.

> God's purpose for us can only be uncovered in Him.

Whether you know your seasonal purpose for right now, or you're struggling to grasp the magnitude of your all-weather purpose, remember that God simply desires a life submitted to Him. Your identity is not in who you are; it's in who He is. It's not what you do; it's what He did. It's not where you live; it's where He dwells.

UNDERSTANDING OUR DIFFERENT PURPOSES

The book of Jeremiah introduces a man by the same name, known as a prophet to the nations. In the first chapter of the book, God unveils Jeremiah's purpose, but it's neither simple nor straightforward. God tells Jeremiah that in his lifetime he will be assigned one all-weather purpose and six seasonal ones.

Some people will tell you that discovering your purpose will often happen in hindsight, after much reflection. But notice how God revealed Jeremiah's purpose before he even set out to fulfill it. The important thing to note is that Jeremiah was already in conversation with God. His purpose was uncovered in his relationship

ZIMISM

Change doesn't
start with planting;
it begins with
uprooting.

with God. If we study Jeremiah's seasonal purposes even more, we find that they exist in stages: two that involve uprooting from a foundation, two that involve destruction, and the final two that involve rebuilding.

What God ultimately requires of us can't be completed in a few months or even a few years. Part of it can be, but if we are continually striving to be more like Christ, then our purposes will likely evolve with the seasons as we continue to grow with Him. While we'll likely spend our early years in the faith discovering what it means to live for God, for many of us it will ultimately take brokenness to find our purpose in Him.

Each of us will have different purposes, seasonal or otherwise. Some may be commissioned with an all-weather purpose to unite a nation of people. But in order to fulfill a purpose that grand, there will likely be smaller, seasonal purposes to challenge, test, and strengthen. I imagine that during a few of Jeremiah's seasonal purposes he was hated, maybe even taunted. And yet he persevered. In the seasons where he united everyone, I'm sure he delighted in the fragrance of appreciation, praise, and promotion. The smaller pictures add up to the bigger one. As you run on mission, remember your commitment to the process when things get tough. Run with the same fervor when things look dismal. We don't rest on the laurels of others, we stand on the promises of God.

> For many of us, it will ultimately take brokenness to find our purpose in Him.

To be set over nations and kingdoms, reconstruction was necessary. He needed to restore order to the people. He had to create new systems for managing a government, likely establishing welfare systems that protected residents and travelers. In this process of restoration, I'm sure that he had to lay new foundations and set new rules for ensuring justice and righteousness.

Anytime someone disrupts a system, it causes unrest. In Jeremiah's case, he would have to endure the hatred of his people to fulfill who God called him to be.

God has grand purposes for each of us too. Sometimes we short-change ourselves when we believe that we can't be used mightily by God. The purpose of many heroes of the Bible was grand and beyond the comprehension of the person to whom the purpose was assigned. In perhaps feats of blind faith, these individuals held on to the promises of God—that He was faithful. That He would provide. That He had their best interests at heart.

Anytime someone disrupts a system, it causes unrest.

God knows the plan He's laid before you. He knows the desires of your heart. He knows you by name, and He wants to shift your purpose from finding glory in *your* own name to finding purpose in *His* name.

When God changed someone's name, it was often because He was giving him or her a new identity—one that was directly connected with that person's purpose. "No longer shall your name be called Abram, but your name shall be Abraham; for I have made you a father of many nations. I will make you exceedingly fruitful; and I will make nations of you, and kings shall come from you" (Genesis 17:5–6 NKJV).

Abraham went from being known as a *high father* to a *father of multitudes* when God changed his name from Abram to Abraham. Abraham's wife's name was changed from Sarai, *my princess*, to Sarah, *mother of nations*.

In the New Testament, Saul had been a persecutor of God's people. But when God

ZIMISM

God's purpose
for you will
cancel who
you thought
you were.

changed his name to Paul, he took on a new identity as a disciple of Jesus. In each case, in both the New and Old Testaments, a name change symbolized a new vision that God had instilled in an individual or a new role that He wanted him or her to play in the kingdom.

Has God given you a purpose that you don't yet understand? Your mission isn't to ignore what you've heard until it all makes sense; it's to run in blind faith toward your current assignment.

When God told Abraham to move, he moved. When God told Moses to lead, he led—albeit hesitantly. When Jesus told His disciples to wait for His return, they waited—even when they didn't understand. All in blind faith. God has qualified you because He created you. And He has made you bold. He makes you brave. There are generations who are awaiting your obedience.

When we all have the opportunity to walk in a God-ordained identity, we become singularly focused on who God declares us to be.

Before I got married, my last name—Ugochukwu—carried an identity that could be found scattered across magazines, interviews, and publications. I was proud of what I had accomplished, but I wasn't so proud of who I had become. My identity was tied in what I *did* and not in who God called me to *be*.

I didn't know it then, but there was an entire ministry that could only be born when no one knew who I was—when Internet searches showed empty pages and irrelevant results. I was given a new last name—Flores—when I married my husband. Along with this new name came

I didn't know it then, but there was an entire ministry that could only be born when no one knew who I was.

a new role and purpose in my life: to become a godly wife and partner. For many, our role in God's ministry can only begin in anonymity.

There is new purpose in a new identity. There are profound challenges and beautiful blessings. There is a deeper burden and a holier call. While marriage may not be the way that God chooses to change your identity, it's a reminder that everyone who is effective for the Kingdom of God undergoes an identity change. It's a normal yet often neglected part of living for God. He will transform you—not just once but over and over again.

An all-weather purpose, by definition, is designed to operate and be usable in any type of season. By contrast, a seasonal purpose exists only for a season but plays to the larger all-weather one.

For so long travel was my identity. I thrived in being able to explore the world and teach others how to do the same. It's the badge I wore on my sleeve. I now understand that the company I built and the work that I did had a bigger purpose of its own, one that reached far beyond me. I've always had a gift for challenging old mindsets; the work that I did with Travel Noire tested long-held stereotypes and helped people think differently about their place in the world.

For so long travel was my identity.

It's easy to think that as your seasonal purposes change, your identity naturally should transform as well. Right? Not quite. If you go—like Jeremiah, for example—from tearing down a city to building it up, there will be a general sentiment change among the people. You may go from being the most hated person in the city to the most loved. And if your identity was attached to the satisfaction of the people, you may find yourself making concessions

to please the people instead of doing the uncomfortable thing you were called to do. You may find that your actual mission becomes a watered-down shell of its former, more potent self.

When God changes our name, transforms our identity, and brings us out of a season and into a new one, the most important thing to remember is that we are His. We are not our circumstances. Successful or not, we belong to God. Who we are should be subject to His Word. Everything that we think we are can be found within the pages of the Bible. His Word is our key to knowing Him deeply and intimately. The Bible is the revelation of God's Will; as we spend more time with Him, we will find that in every storm, at every crossroad, in the midst of every trial or triumph, who we are is who God says we are.

We are loved.

We are protected.

We are worthy.

We are purposed.

We are made in His image.

We are redeemed.

We are His.

We are free.

God is sovereign in all that He does. While it is impossible for me to tell you what your outcome may be, rest in knowing that your obedience could

save nations—whether you are alive to see it or not. Our purposes have eternal impact, and not only do they require our discipline, they will also require our boldness.

A few years ago I came across a story about an explorer by the name of Sir Ernest Shackleton who, on his search for men to travel with him to the South Pole, wrote, "Men and women wanted for hazardous journey. Small wages. Bitter cold. Long months of complete darkness. Constant danger. Safe return doubtful. Honor and recognition in case of success."

> Our purposes have eternal impact, and not only do they require our discipline, they will also require our boldness.

When we consider the reward for our obedience, we will inevitably—as humans do—err to seek honor and recognition. However, the journey through each season of our lives may look a lot like what Sir Ernest Shackleton desired of a crew. We will be broken. We will stumble. We may feel like we're unable to forge ahead. We may not even accomplish all that God desires us to. But when we stand face to face with the One who created us, and the burden of our former life melts away, it will be our heart of obedience that necessitates a "well done" from our faithful Creator (Matthew 25:23).

QUESTIONS FOR REFLECTION

Identifying your seasonal purpose will require reflection and tracking, which I share in more detail in an upcoming chapter. For now, consider the following questions:

1. What traits and gifts do you believe God has given you to impact His Kingdom?

2. What has God revealed to you regarding your all-weather purpose and/or your seasonal purposes?

3. What new identity is the Lord trying to get you to grab hold of?

2/
SELAH

I HELD MY BREATH.

My boyfriend and I had been talking about it for weeks, but honestly, I had hoped he'd forgotten about it. I slowly sauntered through the aisles of my favorite store, pausing in front of a line of curly haircare products.

"I think we should take that break," he suggested.

I paused and took a deep breath. "Okay," I hesitantly replied.

"We both need some time away to make sure that we're hearing from God regarding our next steps."

"How long?"

"I'm thinking four weeks of no talking, followed by three weeks of text only. So seven weeks total."

We set a date and stuck to it: July 11, 2017.

When we had our last conversation just before midnight, I began pacing the streets of Monroe Park in Washington, D.C. And then the clock struck midnight. There I was, alone. My safety net robed in human flesh, now gone.

I cried aloud to the LORD, and he answered me from his holy hill. *Selah.*

PSALM 3:4

Little did I know that God would use those seven weeks to orchestrate a radical shift in my life that would allow me to start over. The safety that I had found in my life just twenty-four hours prior would never again exist.

A few days after the beginning of our temporary break, my world began shifting. One bad product launch led to the prospect of either raising more capital for my business or making the difficult decision to sell. I spent weeks oscillating between babbling tears and steady composure. I was failing miserably. And to make matters worse, I couldn't speak to the one person who knew me best. The most important decision of my life would be made without the person who held my security in his hands. At the end of the four weeks, the decision was final: I was selling the company.

ZIMISM

God will
orchestrate
circumstances
to force your
pause.

But would I have really made the decision to sell if I bounced this idea off of him beforehand? Probably not. You see, God orchestrated this painful season in my life to bring me to a single moment of solitude—a pivotal decision-making moment. And in that moment, He tested me. I would either run or stand.

———

God orchestrated this painful season in my life to bring me to a single moment of solitude.

The word *selah* is mentioned roughly seventy-four times in the Bible. Although its exact meaning is unknown, many scholars agree that its meaning necessitates two things: a pause and a praise.

But I didn't feel like praising.

One by one, the team with whom I had built my successful company began to submit their resignation letters. Their faith in my leadership had all but diminished. My decision to keep our business small meant that we weren't exploring new channels at a fast-enough pace, and my desire to keep a business centered on Christ wasn't working either.

I was stubborn. A perfectionist even. My leadership training, despite my best efforts, wasn't sticking. And as hard as I tried, I felt like no one understood me. If I truly wanted to build something God-centered, I had to give up what wasn't.

In a little under sixty days, the papers were signed. The deal was done. I no longer owned the company I started. In the months that followed, everything that my team had worked so hard to build became unrecognizable. I felt isolated and alone, with no one to talk to. I went through one of the greatest transformations of my life during this time, and all I could do was retreat and reflect on my failures and what I could have done differently—or what I might do differently now if given the chance.

I had given up what had been the most important marker of my identity for the past four years. Even though what I did was a sacrifice unto God, the darkest period of my life didn't feel like an apt reward. I gave up my security. I felt abandoned by industry friends. I felt like less of myself than ever. And as much as I wanted out of the struggle, I stayed.

If I truly wanted to build something God-centered, I had to give up what wasn't.

DON'T GUT THE FISH

The book of Jonah chronicles a man of the same name who rebelled against the instructions of God and fled from Nineveh. He was tossed into a tumultuous sea, only to be swallowed by a giant fish that God had appointed. Inside the fish's belly, Jonah was faced with a decision: he could either force his way out of the fish—gutting it from the inside out—or he could embrace the stillness.

The situation couldn't have been comfortable for Jonah. It was probably terrifying. He probably felt stranded, trapped on all sides even. But as he prayed to God, he didn't pray for deliverance, like many would have.

It was only while being still, inside the fish, that he received revelation. There he was, trapped in the belly of this creature for three days and three nights. Instead of trying to escape, he made a declaration. He acknowledged his own short-comings and thanked God, offering up a sacrifice of praise and proclaiming that God had the final say. Salvation belonged to Him.

> Instead of trying to escape, he made a declaration.

In times like these, it's important that we don't find ourselves desiring deliverance more than revelation. Sometimes, when we don't understand what's happening around us, we just want the pain to stop. We want to press fast-forward on the season we're currently in. We want to jump to the place where we already have the success, the money, and the prestige. We also want it without the pain, discomfort, or effort. Without the tears. Without the loneliness and isolation. But wanting out too early simply evades the process that God wants us to go through. It eliminates the growth we'll experience if we stay the course.

Jonah fled God's instruction because he knew that He was compassionate. He knew that God would forgive a nation that was wicked against Him. But it was that same compassion that led to his sympathetic prayer inside the belly of the fish. Joseph, a man of God sold into slavery by his brothers, could interpret dreams. It was this same gift that allowed him to rise to power in the land of his affliction.

God has given each of us traits that we can use during hard times. There are countless examples of men and women of God being put to the test. But what is most noble and notable about their stories isn't of their escape; it's what happened when they endured. God has proven over and over that He will bless our endurance. He sees exactly what we're going through and will respond at just the right time.

ZIMISM

The work that
God wants to do
in us requires
both our pause
and our praise.

And as much as we desire the rescue, we have to find comfort in the discord. The Bible tells us in Isaiah 66:9 that God will not cause pain without something new being born. It is in the stillness of the storm that we will find peace.

It's in the early mornings alone.

It's in our quiet time with the Lord.

It's in the silent sobs.

Refusing to gut the fish means that we're committed to the assignment God has for us. It's saying to God, "I know You brought me to this new place; I refuse to move back home." It's declaring that the goodness God has for us is just on the other side of the mission.

> It is in the stillness of the storm that we will find peace.

When Jonah was delivered from the belly of the fish, he wasn't regurgitated into the ocean to fend for himself. He didn't have to swim miles back to shore. Even though he was tossed into the ocean in the middle of a storm, Jonah was delivered onto the safety of the shore. Jonah was delivered on firm ground with a fresh revelation of his assignment. "Then the word of the LORD came to Jonah the second time, saying, 'Arise, go to Nineveh, that great city, and call out against it the message that I tell you'" (Jonah 3:1–2).

THE DARKEST HOURS

Even in our darkest hours, we are still under the protection of the Lord. We will never understand our purpose if we always gut the fish. Even Jesus retreated into solitude. And when He was tempted by the devil, He didn't run. He stayed, eventually fulfilling His purpose.

What would have happened if I had gone running back to my boyfriend during our break? As godly a man as he was, God didn't need

ZIMISM

Your
God-given
gifts will make
room for
unexpected
pockets of grace
for when you
need it most.

someone else clouding my judgment or testing my obedience. He needed me to stay put and trust in His sovereignty.

If I hadn't obeyed God and made that tough decision to sell, I wouldn't be writing this book. I wouldn't have had the crisis of faith that led me to a deeper relationship with Him. I wouldn't be free from the opinions of other people. I wouldn't have stayed in Chicago. And I wouldn't have the depth and meaning in my marriage that I do now.

All that the Lord blessed me with was a direct result of my commitment to staying in the belly of the fish—not begging for deliverance but thanking God for the blessings to come. I thank Him—not for the hardship but for the assignment.

Choosing not to gut the fish is perhaps the most grueling part of it all. We know that God sees what's happening, and sometimes it seems like cruel and unusual punishment. But how else will God grow us? Certainly not by laying out His entire plan in front of our eyes.

BLINDSIDED

When I was selling my company, I felt blindsided. It was earlier than I had planned on selling—in fact, if it were up to me, I'd still have it. But I knew I had to retreat—to take a walk in the wilderness. I spent hours each day in tears, but I also prayed for God to keep me there for as long as He needed.

Was it an easy season in my life? No. Am I better for staying exactly where He needed me? Absolutely.

Where you are right now is ordained.

Where you are right now is ordained. You're there because it's exactly where God needs you to be, and the outcome of this season will depend on your obedience. If we run every time things get hard, we'll end up missing the season that God is using to develop us.

Can you imagine how Jonah must have felt with the weight of a nation on his shoulders? And how the people's fate hinged on his obedience? Maybe he longed for simpler times, perhaps where his decisions didn't affect so many people.

No matter how painful or how terrified we are of the unknown, we have to remember that our former lives weren't necessarily better. They were just different. When we find ourselves dwelling on the simpler days, we should remember Isaiah 43:18–19, which says, "Remember not the former things, nor consider the things of old. Behold, I am doing a new thing; now it springs forth, do you not perceive it? I will make a way in the wilderness and rivers in the desert."

> We are being refined.

We are being refined. We are growing. And even though the process is painful, it's important to stay in it. Eventually we'll get to the promise. Because it *is* promised. Those who stayed in the midst of their challenges benefitted from a full restoration of God's promise in their lives.

Joseph was a dreamer who was sold into slavery, but later became a ruler over Egypt.

Job had everything taken from him, but never cursed God. In the end, his riches were completely restored—and then some.

David was a shepherd boy who became the king of Israel.

Esther was an orphan who became a queen.

And Rahab was a prostitute who became an ancestress of Jesus Christ.

When God delivered Jonah, He did it unto his purpose—a calling to rebuke the people of Nineveh who had sinned against God. God wants to deliver us unto our purpose, but it's up to us to stay the course.

Within the quiet moments of a tumultuous season, you'll find the answers you need—as long as you don't force your way out. Pause and praise. We can't pray our way out of a silent season. But we can pray for the strength

to endure and for an open heart to receive. That's how we make it out to the glory of God.

———

Sure, I could have gutted the fish and found an easy way out of my situation. I could have fired my team to cut costs. I could have taken a bridge from investors. I could have even launched a new product.

But it was my willingness to stay in a posture of surrender that meant that what I did next—selling a business on which I had built my identity—proved to God that He could trust me with whatever He held for me next.

I couldn't help but think about David. I wondered if he felt like pausing and praising God when he was running from a man who wanted him dead. He was living in a nightmare. He was constantly on the run. But still he found time to pause and praise. If in his darkest hour he found God to still be good and worthy of praise despite the circumstance, what made me any different? Why couldn't I see God's sovereignty in the middle of my mess? Why didn't I recognize when God was rearranging my life for good?

God is a character-forming God. He turns our times of transition into testimonies for His glory. A simple pause and praise transforms our distress into powerful revelations. The moment I stood in the belly of what I faced and turned my pause into a praise, the easier it became to let my old identity go. I began to thank God for the pain because the pause was necessary to activate the praise.

Selah then becomes the conduit by which we learn to appreciate the many transitions of

———

A simple pause and praise transforms our distress into powerful revelations.

———

ZIMISM

In the middle
of trouble, what
we recognize
from God as
harm, He sees
as good.

life, whether planned or not. The Bible tells us that all things work together for the good of those who are called according to His purpose (Romans 8:28). When we think about the goodness of God, we cannot fully do so without pausing to reflect on the many ways that He has shaped our lives and saved us from the devices of the enemy.

While the pause may be forced, the praise may not feel natural—and that's okay.

When we pause and focus on what's happening *to* us, we miss why it's happening *for* us.

It's easy to pause and complain. It's easier to pause and sulk. The Israelites, on their journey from Egypt to the Promised Land, reacted the same way. "From Mount Hor they set out by the way to the Red Sea, to go around the land of Edom. And the people became impatient on the way. And the people spoke against God and against Moses, 'Why have you brought us up out of Egypt to die in the wilderness? For there is no food and no water, and we loathe this worthless food'" (Numbers 21:4–5).

> When we pause and focus on what's happening *to* us, we miss why it's happening *for* us.

Their complaining and plain disobedience kept them from the Promised Land. Their journey was supposed to take only eleven days. Instead it took forty years! No matter what incredible miracles the Lord brought before them, they continued to complain.

The moment praise dwells on our lips, God is in the midst. The Bible says that God inhabits the praises of His people (Psalm 22:3). If we truly want God near us during the times when we need Him most, it's important to develop a posture of praise, no matter the circumstance.

Not sure how you'll pay your bills this month? Pause and praise Him for what you know He will do (even if it seems impossible).

Moved to a new city and having trouble making new friends? Pause and praise God that your time in isolation is allowing you to build a deeper, more dependent relationship with Him.

Did you end things with a significant other and you're struggling to find your way? Pause and praise God for the room He's now made for a healthy relationship to grow in His perfect timing.

You see, pausing and praising doesn't just change our hearts, it transforms our minds. When we thank Him for the things He's already done, what He has chosen not to do in our lives begins to fade into the distance.

Selah isn't just for us; it's also for those around us. As representatives of Christ, when we are bold in our declaration of God's goodness and faithfulness, even when things feel like they're crumbling around us, we signal to others that our faith transcends our circumstances.

> Pausing and praising doesn't just change our hearts, it transforms our minds.

And the reality is that faith in the middle of suffering looks a lot different than faith in the testimony. Faith during our testimony is polished. It speaks of an undeniable, unshakable faith in the goodness of God and His sovereignty. But faith in the middle of our suffering asks questions. It doubts. It can be angry. As we go through new challenges, we realize that faith isn't pretty. It's ugly. It's hard. It can break us. And our lack of it can turn us away from God.

Faith requires a pause. And let's be honest: no one likes waiting. We wait for our Uber drivers, we wait for coffee at Starbucks, we wait for browsers to load when we're connected to slow Internet. We wait in long lines. We wait in traffic. We wait for the perfect relationship. We wait months for our babies to arrive. Pausing without praising leaves room for the enemy to introduce tactics of deceit and confusion. An idle mind breeds more contempt.

Think about what we'll be able to do for God's Kingdom if we master the art of pausing and praising. You have assignments that are meant just for you. I have responsibilities that are meant just for me.

Selah means that we are actively positioning ourselves to receive God's best. It means that we acknowledge God's direction and timing in our lives. Faith is important. In fact, the Bible says that it is impossible to please God without it (Hebrews 11:6). Imagine your life if during every trial you had absolute confidence that God was with you. Or imagine your response if you knew God was working within the details to leverage everything for your good.

> *Selah* means that we are actively positioning ourselves to receive God's best.

Faith grows from being tested and enduring. We grow from faith to faith; we don't just magically start with tons of faith in God. According to Romans 12:3, God gives everyone a measure of faith. As Christians, it is then our responsibility to continue to grow in it.

In Luke 5:1–11, Jesus stepped into Simon's boat at Lake Gennesaret so that He could address the crowd of people near the lake's edge. He was looking for a stage. Jesus didn't ask Simon if He could use his boat. Jesus needed a stage so that those crowding around the edge of the lake could see and hear Him.

Simon's boat was in the right place at the right time because of one reason: he didn't get what he thought he wanted when he wanted it. As we later learn in Scripture, Simon had spent the night before trying to catch fish but was unsuccessful. Later that day, when Jesus came to Simon's boat, Simon was properly positioned to be used.

Had Simon been successful and caught fish the night before, he wouldn't have been available for Jesus since he may have been away, selling fish at the market or preoccupied with something else.

If God gave us what we wanted when we thought we needed it, would we still be an available stage for Him? Would we be preoccupied? Would we corrupt what He gives us? Would our pause be filled with something other than His praise?

Sometimes waiting on His timing means removing the things we desire so that we can actually be available to Him during our appointed time.

After Jesus delivered His message to the crowd, and after He told Simon to drop his net, Simon received the very thing he wanted—a catch—but it only came at the right time: after he was obedient and after he was available to be used. God's timing was perfect.

Selah means that your praise is actually an act of faith. It's as if you're saying to God, "Yes, I believe that You will deliver me from this. Yes, I believe

that my latter shall be greater than my former. Yes, I believe that You are working everything out for my good. Yes, I believe that You are preparing me for whatever will come next."

Your pause isn't passive; it's active. It's confident. It's expectant. It's disciplined. It's uncomfortable. It reminds us to cling to God with all we've got.

This is not to say that there is always a reward for your pause and your praise. Perhaps it simply means that God will change your heart about that very thing you thought you wanted. When Jesus and the disciples were in a boat that was caught in a big storm, Jesus

took a nap while the disciples were beside themselves. They woke Him up to ask Him to save them. Matthew 8:26 says, "And he said to them, 'Why are you afraid, O you of little faith?' Then he rose and rebuked the winds and the sea, and there was a great calm."

By sleeping through the storm, Jesus was saying that we can trust Him even in the middle of it. When we pause without praising, we become hasty. We get impatient. We try to take matters into our own hands to try and help God out. What if the disciples had taken a pause and praised the presence of God?

When we choose to stay where God places us, we continue to work as unto the Lord, prioritizing our relationship with Him as we serve others. When we start over in God's Will, He blesses us, even though we may not see it. And He'll bless everyone around us simply because they associate with us.

It may not be our fault that we're in a given situation. It's not our responsibility to figure out what got us there. But it *is* our responsibility to bloom where God plants us—if we dare. Everything that we go through is meant for the greater assignment that He has for us: to be more like Him. His plans for us are as wide as the sky—and unlocking them is a matter of persistence, humility, and obedience. If our life is a staircase and Jesus is on the top step, with every gutted fish, we take a step backward. But God holds us there in His grace. We are already redeemed by His blood. And with every season we stay in the belly of the fish, we take a step toward our purpose.

It *is* our responsibility to bloom where God plants us—if we dare.

QUESTIONS FOR REFLECTION

1. Are you currently going through a trial? What could you do to "gut the fish" and escape your current situation?

2. What traits or habits has God given you that could be useful during a tough season or time of transition?

3. What skills or traits have you developed as a result of staying in the belly of the fish?

4. Take a moment to pause. What can you praise God for—right here, right now?

5. What are three ways that you can shift your perspective about your circumstance?

6. Who does God say you are in the middle of what you're going through?

3/

FRESH
OIL

> But you have
> exalted my horn like
> that of the wild ox;
> you have poured
> over me fresh oil.
>
> **PSALM 92:10**

I LET OUT A DEEP SIGH as I approached the intersection. Burdened by my current set of circumstances, my eyes skimmed over the crowded crossroad and landed on an unsuspecting road sign. I looked up and to the left—a playful habit I developed whenever I felt the Lord speak to me regarding something I was going through. Two words brought all the stressful thoughts running through my mind to a sudden halt: *Fresh Oil.*

How could a road sign so accurately depict my exact circumstance?

———

Thousands of years ago, fresh oil was used with a specific blend of spices to anoint a person for a chosen purpose. When someone was anointed with oil, it was as if God Himself was staking claim on a life. Not only was it a physical recognition of God's calling on that person, but it also symbolized a transfer of holiness from God.

And it wasn't simply a little dab of oil that symbolized this transfer. Oil had to fully run over a person—from the top of their head, through their hair, down their face, and eventually dripping from the hem of their garment. In other words, when God chose a vessel, He went all in. There was no mistake.

An anointing was always preceded by spiritual posture. Had that person made room for God? Had he or she been willing to sacrifice everything

for God's purpose? The level of one's anointing depended on his or her level of consecration and position of preparation. Everything set apart for God was to be anointed, and to be anointed was to become holy and mightily used of God. In the Bible, David was anointed to slay giants. Priests, prophets, and kings were anointed to lead their people.

And *you* are anointed for your purpose.

For summers on end, the Fresh Oil signs often appeared on the corners of intersections, in some variation, around the world. Workers would haul heavy machinery, spraying a thick, lacquerlike oil over the roadway to seal the surface and repair minor cracks during the season that best supported this. You wouldn't see fresh oil being poured during the winter. The fresh oil applied during the warm summer months provided protection not only against wind, rain, and snow, it also prevented the pavement from aging. As everyday road activity happened—tires treading over the asphalt, skid marks peppering the roadway, and tons of metal racing then resting in between the lanes—the pavement suffered no harm because it was sealed.

> And *you* are anointed for your purpose.

But what happens if, over time, new oil isn't reapplied? The earth shifts. Cracks appear. Potholes form. What was once sturdy and resilient is now weakened.

Oil that is stagnant eventually becomes stale. To be effective for the Kingdom, we must constantly be renewed. That means fresh challenges, new heartaches, and painful circumstances that push us desperately closer to God.

The best olive oil is made from olives that are plucked just before they are fully ripe—when they aren't quite ready to be used. There's something special that happens when we, like unripe

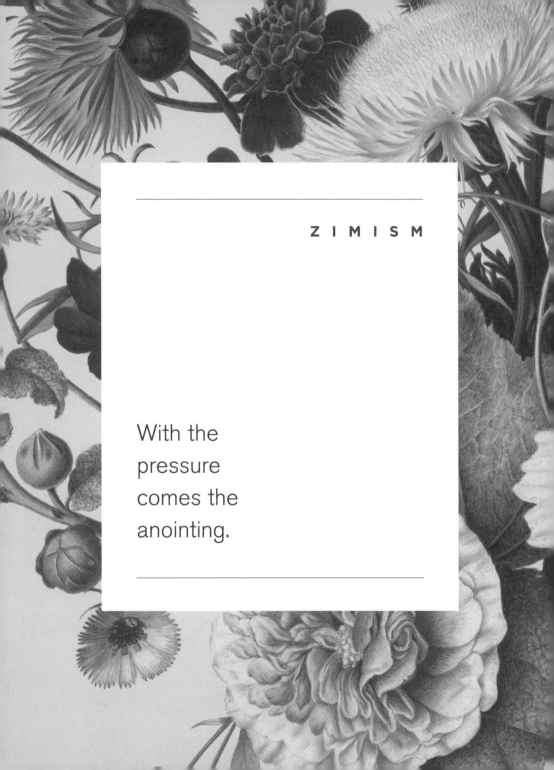

ZIMISM

With the
pressure
comes the
anointing.

olives, feel trapped and pressed on all sides. The coveted oil is produced. The crushing produces character, allowing us to speak powerfully and boldly about what God has delivered us from. But to be delivered, we have to endure the tension.

Back in my car at that intersection, looking up at the sign, I knew what I wanted. I wanted to walk with power over my circumstances. I wanted to live in abundance. I wanted to know exactly who I was, especially when everything was being pulled out from under me. I wanted to defy who society thought I should be.

But I also wanted a comfortable life. I certainly *didn't* want new challenges to shake my identity. I wanted the ease of a life without pain—a life marked by the grace of a ballerina—because let's be honest: ease is a luxury. No one greatly used by God chose comfort over consecration.

Over the next eighteen months, I would burn through my entire savings after uprooting my life in San Francisco and temporarily resettling in the town where I grew up. I would be pressed for an anointing that I didn't know was coming.

> I would be pressed for an anointing that I didn't know was coming.

In all honesty, I shouldn't have been surprised. After all, uprooting was something I should have known intimately.

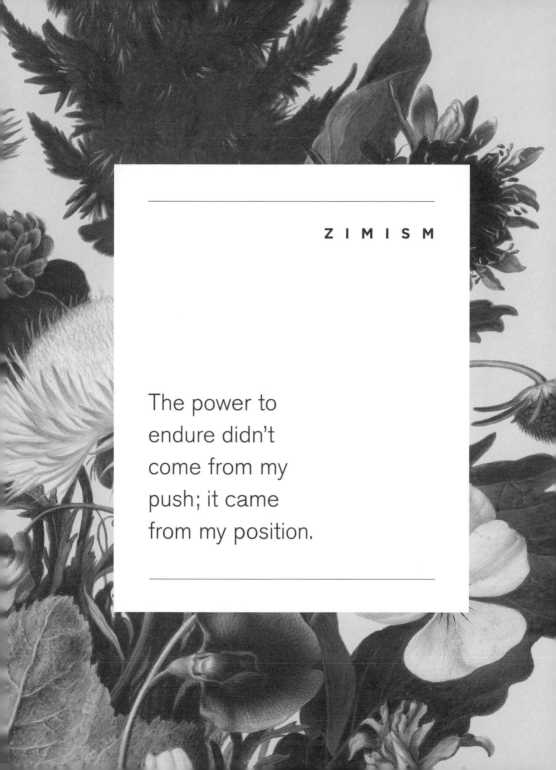

ZIMISM

The power to
endure didn't
come from my
push; it came
from my position.

The year was 2011. I had fallen into a bout of mild depression.

I had just sold everything that I owned and moved across the world to India—far from anyone I knew. I couldn't properly speak the language. I had trouble finding a church. I had no friends. I was an infant in a foreign land.

This time in my life should have felt victorious and adventurous. Up until that point, though, my identity was wrapped around the accolades and trophies that had qualified me for the fellowship that had sent me to India. And while it was an exciting transition, I found myself in a place where none of that mattered. Now I was simply one in a billion. I felt invisible. And I barely recognized who I was.

I was twenty-three years old and had gone from being one of the most recognized faces on my campus to fielding unwanted curious stares every day. Loneliness penetrated my heart and felt like a dense cloud that followed me to work each day. My deepest fear was that I was losing relevance. My status to the outside world held more power in my heart than my status with Christ.

> My deepest fear was that I was losing relevance.

I felt desperate. And I wanted to go home.

As uncomfortable as it was, I knew that if I wanted to become a better person, I couldn't force my way out of what God was trying to teach me. I needed the fresh oil to restore my memory. Although I thought I knew what I wanted, the fresh oil that I needed was the challenge to build my character and transform my life to mirror Christ's.

The power to endure didn't come from my push; it came from my position.

My job was to trust that God's plan was good and that His grace would be sufficient enough to carry me. And now? I can speak boldly about what the Lord delivered me from. Through Him, I have the power to overcome new challenges.

ZIMISM

Difficult times
reveal the
priorities of
our hearts.

I've discovered through those times something I hold with me each time I feel a new beginning coming: with every change in my environment or shift in my life, I grow sharper and bolder. My unique gifts continue to unfold as God changes my surroundings.

You may have lost your job. Your husband may have walked out on you. Someone you loved may have passed away. Your friends may have betrayed you. You may have ended a meaningful relationship. You may currently find yourself in the middle of an uprooting.

I may not have the words to make your pain disappear, but I do have hope to share that will give you peace along the journey. It may not get easier right away, but you'll get better. You'll get stronger. You'll become more resilient. Whatever new place you find yourself in right now, God wants to pour fresh oil over you to remove, remind, and restore.

He wants to remove the things that hinder your growth. The friendships that don't serve your destiny. That toxic relationship. The small mindset. He wants to remind you that your identity is not rooted in what you lost. You are not what happened to you. You are His. He wants to restore you beyond your former glory. You thought life was good before? In Him it will be even better. This fresh oil means that your future victories are sealed by Him. All you have to do is stay close to Him.

Perhaps you were like me, living life on cruise control, and you felt like God plucked you from your otherwise comfortable circumstance, uprooting you before your prime. Isn't it beautiful that He assigns us to hard times when we least expect it? He blesses us with the burden that will elevate us. Whatever happens to us isn't because God is punishing us; it's because He is protecting us.

Sometimes you may feel like you're in over your head. God's promise isn't to make things easier; it's to make you more like Him.

Change is painful—but it can also feel exciting if you let it, knowing that God is in control. And perhaps there is no feeling more daunting than starting over—being stripped of the power of familiarity. But here's the truth: God wants to trust you. And He wants to trust that you'll be faithful to the lessons of this new time and place.

I may not understand exactly what you're going through. But I know that walking in the light of God has one common denominator: facing hard things. Grain, wine, and oil are mentioned together many times in the Bible. It is of no coincidence that to harvest these valuable commodities, each needs to be pressed and crushed to reveal its coveted value.

The beginning of any new season isn't marked first by crushing; it's defined by uprooting— an uprooting of your comfort zone, mentality, or mindset, among other things.

We all have a promise. That promise requires us to be in position so that anointing can flow. In Scripture, no one was able to accomplish anything if he or she wasn't in a position to hear from God. Esther, an orphan who rose to become the unlikely queen who saved the Jews from destruction, first fasted, seeking direction from God before executing a plan to save His people.

> The beginning of any new season isn't marked first by crushing; it's defined by uprooting.

David, one of the greatest kings in the Bible, made daily prayer a top priority—even when faced with the toughest of challenges. He knew God's promises stood on firm ground. Moses went from royalty to vagabond because he followed his promise into anointing. Did he want to move? I'm sure he could think of better things to do. But he went from stuttering and being afraid to speak publicly to becoming the mouthpiece of a nation.

I may not be able to tell you much about your specific anointing, but I can tell you that with it you'll walk in power and on mission—and that's all the relevance you'll need. God shows us how to become more like Him.

He tells us to know His Word. We know Him deeply when we learn of His character.

He tells us to engage with those we love; we can encourage them and celebrate life's beautiful transformations.

He tells us to pray without ceasing—the kind of prayer that celebrates who He is and surrenders every fear to Him.

He tells us to participate in the world by giving to the least among us and meeting the needs of those around us. When we celebrate the dignity of others, we elevate His name.

He tells us to go and tell others about who He is, in word and deed. By living fully with God, we get to be partners in the revival to come.

We're on a mission when we're living and loving like Christ. Our anointing will deliver other people. Anointing means less of us and more of Him. It challenges every zone of comfort. It shifts worlds. It transforms lives.

> Our anointing will deliver other people.

And anointing changes the direction of your life. It means you're walking on mission. It means you have something to accomplish and you're willing to sacrifice your life for it. Anointing isn't born in our comfort zone; it's birthed out of pain.

What if the fresh oil that God wants to pour over us isn't a one-time thing? What if it is a continual process, trial after trial? And what if the anointing is only ever wrapped in a painful package? Would we still want it?

If the anointing is what we're after, we have to understand that to be trusted with God's anointing means to be well acquainted with His standard—a life that is set apart for Him. This is not to say that being chosen of God means we will lead painful, miserable lives—quite the opposite. God declares that a life in Him is one of abundance, provision, and protection.

> God declares that a life in Him is one of abundance, provision, and protection.

As you continue to read *Dare to Bloom*, I want to posit a reminder: what you're going through right now isn't happening *to* you—it's happening *for* you. And when you shift your perspective, you'll find that the fresh oil isn't all that bad.

QUESTIONS FOR REFLECTION

1. Are you in the middle of an uprooting in your life?

2. What comforts have you had to give up?

3. How do you think God is using your story for His glory?

4. What fresh oil has God poured over you in this season of your life?

5. Name three character traits you developed in the last challenging season of your life.

4

FROM CUPBEARER TO RULER

THREE HUNDRED MILES INTO THE JUNGLE. A three-hour drive down a dimly lit backroad. A thirty-minute boat ride to an island invisible from the shore.

The more difficult the journey, the more beautiful the arrival.

A few years ago I drove, with a few strangers, from Windhoek, Namibia, to a small peninsula in the northern part of the country. We settled in Caprivi, home to various exotic wildlife. We had a few stops along the way, one at Etosha National Park to view the wildlife, and other stops that were lesser known but equally rich in culture.

> And the angel of the LORD came again a second time and touched him and said, "Arise and eat, for the journey is too great for you." And he arose and ate and drank, and went in the strength of that food forty days and forty nights to Horeb, the mount of God.
>
> **1 KINGS 19:7–8**

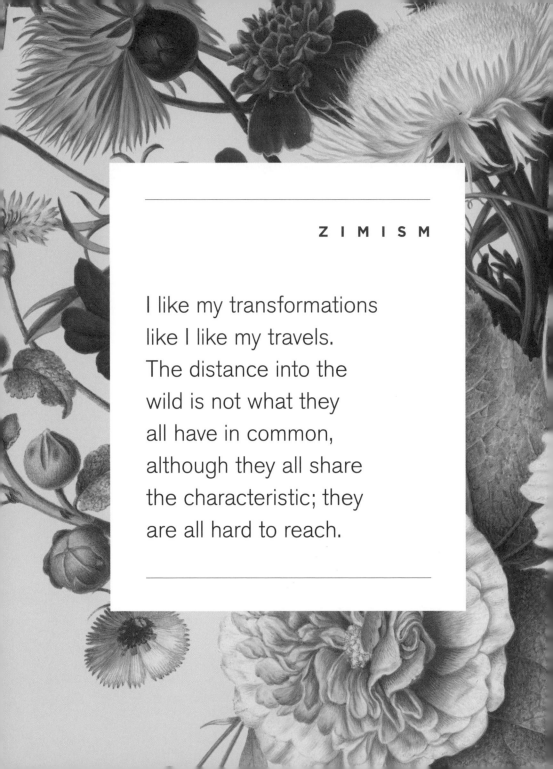

ZIMISM

I like my transformations
like I like my travels.
The distance into the
wild is not what they
all have in common,
although they all share
the characteristic; they
are all hard to reach.

Although the journey was long and I was restless, there were strategic perspective-changing moments along the way:

A wild elephant crossed the abandoned highway, its weighty saunter halting everything in its path.

The empty expressway dressed with brown-butter sand as far as the eyes can see.

The freckled night sky, tiny white doorways that gave way to an expansive reality.

My fear of flying often means that I take to the road more than I would like—which may seem strange for someone who used to own a boutique travel company. A quick two-hour flight back to Windhoek morphed into an eight-hour journey bound by the walls of a far-too-small vehicle.

We pulled up to the airport: a single-lane, backroad-sized runway sandwiched between unkempt grass. Our entire crew was scheduled to board the small plane back to the capital city.

"I'm good. I'll ride back with the team."

All eyes were on me.

"That's a fourteen-hour drive, Zim."

> I took a deep breath, and as reality sank in, I nodded in acceptance.

My heart sank. I knew it would be a long ride, and I already dreaded it. It would be one of those trips without any time to spare. We wouldn't be making any stops, save for an occasional snack and toilet break.

The road trip would be a straight shot from one end of the country to the other. I took a deep breath, and as reality sank in, I nodded in acceptance. I slid the van door open and plopped inside, then looked out of the dust-tinted window to the group I was leaving behind. They were heading on one journey. I, on another.

As we pulled away, disappointment wore like a pin on my sleeve. I had let fear get the best of me. And for so long I let it dictate every decision I made.

Fear wasn't who I was; I simply needed a bold reminder to believe it. Where you're headed may be unchartered territory, and it's natural for the fear of the unknown to sink in. I could wallow in my self-imposed fear-riddled label, or I could relax into the new identity that God was crafting for me: a bold, flawed woman who loved God and strived each day to inspire people to lean into their God-given peculiarities.

Thankfully I had other examples to remind me.

> Fear wasn't who I was; I simply needed a bold reminder to believe it.

———

Nehemiah was a cupbearer with a healthy fear of the Lord and a strong conviction to rebuild the city wall in Jerusalem. As a cupbearer, he delighted in a special kind of closeness to the king. After all, he was responsible for tasting the wine served to the king as a precaution against poisoning. When he left for his journey to Jerusalem, he had no idea what lay ahead.

He had a giant task at hand, a mission and a purpose set just for him. I don't think he thought much about his former identity, even though he knew that he'd have to return one day. The most important thing on his mind was what God had set in his heart to do.

Rebuilding and embarking on new beginnings didn't come without the fear tactics and intimidation strategies from outsiders. But Nehemiah remained undeterred. He knew that his outsider status had no bearing on his future status. He knew that he belonged to God and had confidence in His plan. He communed regularly with God and enjoyed a deep relationship with Him.

Here was a man who put his life on the line every day for someone else—for a king, in this case—and who, over time, was appointed the governor of Judah. Nehemiah's obedience and commitment to God allowed for his elevation from cupbearer to ruler.

The long journey back to Windhoek—and many other rides just like that—was a journey that God needed me to take. My change in identity would come only after spending time in His presence.

My change in
identity would
come only after
spending time
in His presence.

A FORMULA FOR STARTING OVER

One thing I've noticed in Scripture over the years is a specific formula for starting over, according to the Will of God.

1. An event or trigger
2. Knowledge of God and a relationship with Him
3. Position and long-suffering
4. Achieving the promise

First there will be a trigger or an event. For example, Joseph was sold into slavery by his brothers. Esther was made queen. Jonah was swallowed by a fish. Abraham was given a promise.

You'll then notice in every case that there is a relationship with God, whether new or otherwise. When we're in a healthy relationship or have healthy friendships, we exude the fruits of that relationship. Likewise, our relationship with God bears the fruit of godliness and holiness. You can see God and godliness in people by the fruit that they display. Are they kind? Are they patient? Are they loving? Are they gentle? Do they have self-control?

ZIMISM

With
elevation
comes a
change in
identity.

Although God isn't mentioned in the book of Esther, you can see His providence throughout every chapter. He is evident through Esther in her position—the way she carries herself, the way she makes decisions, her responses when faced with a tough decision. This is the third part of the formula. When Esther had the difficult decision of figuring out what to do next after hearing that her people were going to be killed, she did one thing: she called for a fast.

Fasting acknowledges our human frailty before God. It changes us and cultivates wisdom, understanding, and revelation concerning the things of God and His Will. Fasting helps to develop a sensitivity to the presence of God as we align our will with God's. We begin to hear Him clearly. We begin to be directed according to the things of the Spirit, not according to our hearts, our feelings, or our desires. Fasting also allows for the molding and shaping that comes from disciplining our flesh.

David once said that he humbled his soul through fasting (Psalm 35:13). Fasting, coupled with faith in God's Will, made Esther unstoppable. She needed to be in tune to what God wanted her to do, and fasting meant that her flesh couldn't get in the way.

And finally, the promise. Having a relationship with God means that no matter the storm, we have Someone who has us covered. He's our armor. If someone tries to stab us in the back, we have protection. If someone tries to harm us with words, He's our shield. Our relationship with God will fortify us in our seasons of new beginnings.

What if, before wallowing in our own self-pity with regard to who we thought we were, we

> Having a relationship with God means that no matter the storm, we have Someone who has us covered.

went to God first? What if we submitted ourselves through prayer and fasting? How can we cultivate a habit of first seeking God and hearing what He has to say?

As you spend time with God, you will feel an unexplainable joy. There is a peace in knowing that the path of life is in His Word. If we stay with it, when life gets hard, when we're tired, when we feel hopeless, when we're broken, when we're angry, when we have to start over, when our friends turn their backs on us, when people hate us for no reason, God promises that He is with us, always—and the path to abundance is found in Him.

Your past identity has no bearing on what God has planned for your future. Stay in His presence, and you will find that nothing and no one can take away all that He has for you.

1. Have you been afraid to start over because
    of previous roles or labels or because of who
    people said you were? What happened?

2. Can you recall a time when you put more value
    on what other people have said than on what
    God has to say? What did you learn?

3. Why do you think God chooses common people
    to do the extraordinary for His Kingdom?

4. What new role do you feel God leading
    you toward? Are you resisting, or are you
    leaning in? If you're resisting, what
    would it look like to lean in?

5/

WHEN THEY
CAN'T STAY

A FEW HAZY SUMMERS AGO, I LEFT my family compound in Nnewi to drive to Lagos, the largest city in Nigeria. As the driver and I pulled away and the cement gate disappeared in the distance, I began to brace myself for the perilous seven-hour journey ahead.

But only minutes into the ride, he abruptly pulled over, got out of the car, and walked away. A cloud of uncertainty billowed over me. I wondered what the random pit stop was for, but still in an early morning daze, I shrugged it off.

The driver eventually returned with a man who was in need of a ride to Lagos, which, I admit, bothered me. After being in Nigeria for so long, I had become rather defensive about my personal space and interactions with men. *Who was this intruder?*

On long journeys, it wasn't uncommon for this driver to stop and pick up anxious passengers hoping to pay a discounted fare for a semi-private ride. My heart raced as annoyance swelled in my chest.

"I paid for a private ride," I declared with a banner of certainty. "If you want him to come with us, we need to go back to my grandmother's house and let her know that I'm traveling with someone new."

The driver knew my grandmother. She was feisty. Her words could fracture even the burliest of men. He cowered his head with a tinge of shame and quickly recovered to let me know that we wouldn't take the man with us. He slammed the sliding van door in front of him.

The satisfaction that illuminated my face as I leaned back into the seat quickly grew dim as I glanced out of the window. I

> Do not neglect to show hospitality to strangers, for thereby some have entertained angels unawares.
>
> **HEBREWS 13:2**

saw a man defeated. His face aged with the wrinkles of despair. His eyebrows bowed as if to give way for tears to fall. At that moment, the duality of compassion and guilt filled my heart.

The driver started the car. I bore the weight of the world as I opened my door to ask the man to join us. He frantically looked down, fumbling with a crinkled stack of papers as if he had something to prove. He lifted a few for me to see. Medical bill after medical bill. In his desperation, a few receipts managed to slip between his frail fingers and onto the cracked concrete beneath his feet.

> I bore the weight of the world as I opened my door to ask the man to join us.

He had come to pay his wife's medical bills. He frequently made the seven-hour expedition to visit her in the hospital and pay for ongoing care. He didn't have much. His years seemed to subdue him, and I could feel the heaviness of his burden as he opened the passenger door and sat down.

I ached for him. I watched as a spectator, witnessing the unwinnable race he was running. I saw the devastation and hopelessness that would park in the spaces of his heart when his wife could no longer stay with him.

His struggle was also mine.

———

I was supposed to be past this. If bitterness were a substance that flowed freely, I could still feel it coursing through my veins.

My life had been recently changing at breakneck speed, and my close friends were supposed to be my people. However, my career change, coupled with a deep desire to know God, began repelling people all around me. I was frustrated. Beyond the

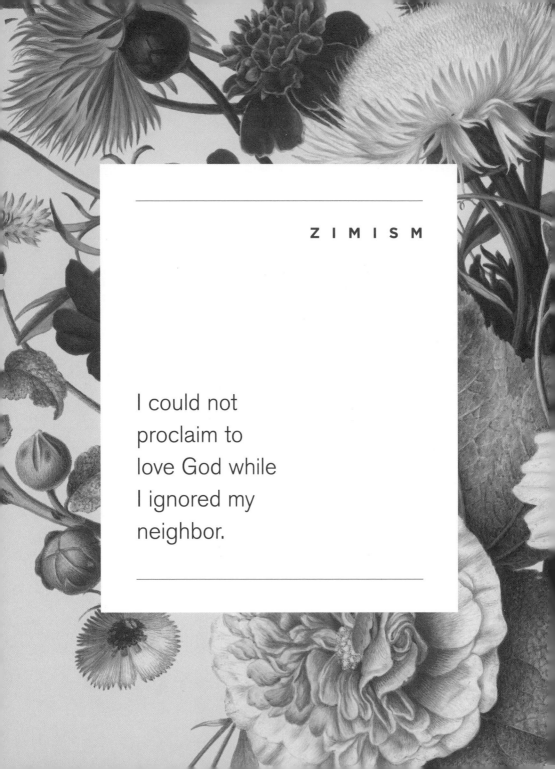

ZIMISM

I could not
proclaim to
love God while
I ignored my
neighbor.

superficial politeness, I could no longer relate. The profound conversations that once felt like home ceased to feel safe. The more God called me near, the more I grew estranged to the people and places all around me. The more God called me near, the more I repelled what I loved.

But if I'm completely honest, my identity—the one that I had so neatly placed in the hands of these friends—was being called to question. I was ready to follow Him but realized that I couldn't force my friends to do the same. As the weight of a new beginning began to unfold, the weak bonds of our friendship were exposed, and all that we had in common fell away. I was left to stand alone.

The more God called me near, the more I repelled what I loved.

And the ugly reality was that I spent much more time placing my worth in the status that came with being close to these successful friends than I did actually building relationships of substance. Phrases laced in rejection and confusion constantly filled my mind. The nagging thoughts just wouldn't go away. No amount of sleep could subdue them. No depth of reflection seemed to heal them. No matter what I did, the more I thought about it, the more the pain was made fresh day after day.

And perhaps the sting of their togetherness pierced the deepest. The laughter. The candor. The celebrations suspended in time. Seeing them with one another nursed an ache so deep, it seemed like a chasm as wide as the sky. The weddings I would never attend. The late-night conversations we would never have. Those sacred moments we would never again share.

They didn't need me. And it sure didn't seem like they missed me. My face suddenly felt warm as tears welled up and fell to temper my cheeks. Eventually they moved on without me, and although I desperately wanted to feel like an insider again, it was clear that I was out.

I was angry. I felt helpless. How dare they move on so easily? Compulsively, I began to stalk their social profiles. Beyond the depths of my nosiness, what I truly yearned for was the identity I lost in their

friendship. I wanted to belong again. It became my focus. But what we let linger, festers.

Although I mourned the worth I found in them, I knew they couldn't stay—although I desperately wanted them to. I had planted the flag of my worth on sinking sand, and as long as my identity rested in other people, I would never stop chasing the sense of belonging.

Identity is complicated. It's messy. It's intangible. And we often wrap up our identities in people who are just as broken as we are. I wish it could be simpler. Perhaps it could be, if we fight deep pain with radical forgiveness. We may be telling ourselves:

I can't forgive this friend because of all she did—or didn't do—in my life.

I can't forgive her because then she'll get away with what she did—I'd be letting her off the hook.

I can't forgive her because I actually don't want her back in my life. I'm happier without her. If I do forgive her, that means I have to reconcile with her.

I can't forgive her because she won't repent or ask for forgiveness. Why extend that forgiveness to someone who doesn't think she's guilty?

I can't forgive her because I don't care about the past. My life is moving forward now, and my energy should be spent on the future.

I can't forgive her because she'll never change. There's no point in trying.

I can't forgive her because I want her to suffer for all of the terrible things she's done to me. Let her enjoy what she's earned.

> As long as my identity rested in other people, I would never stop chasing the sense of belonging.

If this is where you find yourself—in unforgiveness—it's important that you don't stay there. In fact, I believe it's a matter of life and death.

There's one simple reason that you *can* forgive the friends who have hurt you: because God has forgiven you. The Bible tells us that when God forgives us, He tosses our sins into the depth of the sea. We're free.

But that freedom isn't just for us to live a happy and unburdened life. Our freedom is for others. For those who were like us—selfish, lonely, miserable, prideful. It's for people who hurt us. It's for our friends who betray us. It's for the people who talk about us. They need forgiveness as much as you do. And we get to pass it on. We have the privilege of passing on the deep love of God to others. We can offer it to people whom we feel deserve it the least. God loves them—so let's allow Him to love them more through us. To be a witness and a light to others.

> We can pass on the deep love of God to others.

Forgiveness frees us. It heals us. It makes us more like Christ. And learning to forgive helps us control our own narrative, allowing us to choose between living as a victim and living like Christ.

We can acknowledge and feel the full pain of what happened to us. We can feel our feelings without letting them overtake us. But by letting go and choosing to forgive, we're not acknowledging that what they've done to us was okay. We're simply making the choice to not be ruled by it.

I don't have all of the answers, although I wish I did. The only thing that worked for me in healing the sting of a failed friendship was learning to embrace the fringe experience.

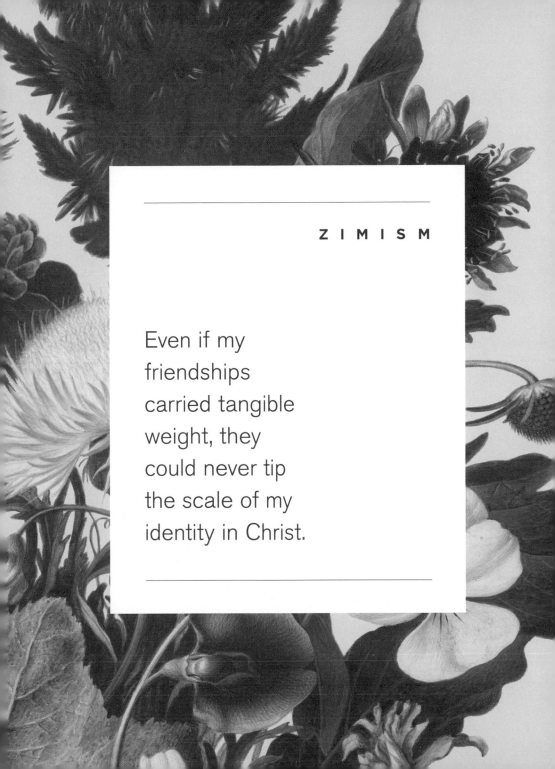

ZIMISM

Even if my
friendships
carried tangible
weight, they
could never tip
the scale of my
identity in Christ.

THE FRINGE EXPERIENCE

In Joshua 2 and 6, there is a woman named Rahab whose very identity was cloaked in the culture and customs of an ancient, sinful society. A Canaanite woman living in Jericho, she made her living as a prostitute—a profession that, in those days, bore a broad banner of tolerance. In a land rife with fertility cults and holy prostitutes, Rahab's identity was an important thread in the tapestry of the nation.

After the death of Moses, God appointed Joshua to lead the people of Israel, who had wandered in the wilderness for forty years, into the land that was promised to them. With the weight of this assignment on his shoulders, Joshua commanded officers to the west of the Jordan River and the people to the east to prepare for the conquest of Jericho. Fortified with double walls that touched the sky, Jericho was the strongest of the walled cities in Canaan.

If I lived thousands of years ago and were the wife of a soldier who donned armor in preparation for this conquest, I might have called it a suicide mission. But isn't it amazing that God would send His people to face a seemingly impossible task just to prove His faithfulness?

Joshua sent two spies to secretly explore the land of Jericho, and off they went from Shittim, crossing over the Jordan River and traversing through the rugged terrain before arriving to the walled city. After sneaking into the city, they entered Rahab's home and stayed there.

When the king of Jericho caught wind that spies had entered into Jericho, he sent a delegation to Rahab's house to ask that they be turned over. However, instead of revealing where she hid them on her roof, she told the group that the spies had left and instructed them to follow in pursuit.

Who we say we are is rooted in what we love. But what happens when who we are and what we love clash? Rahab knew this delegation of men—in fact, I believe that

> Who we say we are is rooted in what we love.

she knew these high-ranking officials well. But still she hid the truth from them.

Later, on the roof, Rahab privately told the spies that she knew the Lord gave them the land of Jericho and that the Lord was God in Heaven above and on earth below. This was a serious thing for a Canaanite to say. Who she was and what she loved were now at odds.

She asked the spies to swear to her by the Lord that they would show kindness to her entire family and spare them from death when they attacked the city. "Our lives for your lives!" the men assured her. All this on two conditions: that she didn't tell authorities and that she tied a scarlet cord near the window so that the Israelites would know whom to save during the conquest.

When the time came, the walls of Jericho collapsed, and the armed Israelite soldiers engaged the Jericho militia in battle. Everything was destroyed except for Rahab's home, and her family was spared.

ZIMISM

When our
relationships serve
our past at the
expense of our
destiny, concealing
our true identity
becomes impossible.

On the trophy shelves of our lives, Rahab isn't the most revered woman in the Bible. Not even close. There's Ruth. There's Mary. There's the Proverbs 31 woman. There are many women we would probably rather append ourselves to.

Perhaps it's because she was a prostitute, or maybe it's because she lied to the king of Jericho and tricked him into pursuing the spies into the unknown, or it's because she selfishly thought to save her own family alone. Whatever the reason, one thing is certain: every future victory depends on our complete obedience. And Rahab's obedience spared a generation.

> Whatever the reason, one thing is certain: every future victory depends on our complete obedience.

Somehow she knew that she couldn't stay in Jericho. Staying would have certainly meant death for her, her family, and any hope of a legacy. Instead she chose to affix herself to the promise of the One she proclaimed as King.

Rahab sacrificed everything that was familiar, much like the man from Lagos who surrendered daily to care for his ailing wife, and a lot like our precious friendships that fall by the wayside during seasons of growth. But God promises victory.

When the walls of Jericho fell flat and the city was devoted to destruction, Rahab and her family were spared and placed outside of the camp of Israel.

Wait. Outside of the camp? On the fringes of what was promised to them?

There they were, witnesses to the complete destruction of the place they called home. A home where well-maintained friendships ceased to exist. The comfort of their years stripped away from them in an instant. All of that to be placed on the outskirts.

If I were Rahab, I might question God. *Why would He do all of that? The trumpets, the destruction, the plunder, and the grand blockbuster-style rescue only to place me and my family outside of the camp and on the edge of my promise?*

I can't imagine how lonely it must have been. Perhaps they bitterly watched from the sidelines as Israel celebrated their victories. Or maybe they passed the time by mourning the comfort of their old identities.

The truth is that elevation requires a downgrade. And in God's economy isolation begets intimacy.

God brings us low to prepare us for the rise, to prepare us for greatness, assigning to us a wilderness experience—perhaps something as painful as losing an entire group of friends—to call us to higher, more fertile ground. He trims the branches of our mindset that tells us we aren't enough until we are bound to the mind of Christ. He shapes the leaves of our security and wipes clean the ugly collectibles we've accumulated over the years. Alone with Him is where we find true victory from the identities of our past.

If you're stuck feeling like every status update and every social media post remind you of the shattered pieces of your former identity, welcome to the fringe experience. I like to think of this experience as a divinely orchestrated period of time, existing between our past and future identities. When all that we know is gone, it gives God an opportunity to minister into our brokenness.

As the dust of those friendships settle, like a banner emerging from the ashes, God will remain. Deep in the hidden parts of our soul, He weans us from the comfort of their presence. Within the chambers of our heart, He infuses a measure of faith. And for the everyday, He gives us a hymn for the haze.

It was only after Rahab and her family spent time on the fringes that they were able to walk in Israel for the rest of their lives. They finally walked in their promise. Rahab was the great-great-grandmother of King David and an ancestress in the genealogy of Jesus Christ.

He gives us a hymn for the haze.

This is why my friends couldn't stay, and it's why yours might not be able to either. God cannot reposition what doesn't move. We need our time on the fringes. I believe that the lessons that God wants to teach us about relationships come through losing the identity we find in our friendships.

Personally, it meant relinquishing the worldly lifestyle I loved so that I could love Him more. I couldn't walk into the camp of my destiny with the relationships of my past. It would have been a legacy death sentence. And in time, just like Rahab, God will give us people to walk with for the rest of our lives—a village for our souls, those who will stick closer than a brother. We simply have to be willing to face the destruction of who we were and live in expectation of the restoration to come.

How do I know? It's promised to us. "And after you have suffered a little while, the God of all grace, who has called you to his eternal glory in Christ, will himself restore, confirm, strengthen, and establish you" (1 Peter 5:10).

I'm not sure what happened to the Nigerian man after we said our goodbyes in Lagos, but our encounter often reminds me of a simple truth: sometimes strangers are the best teachers. They settle who we declare ourselves to be by reconciling who we truly are.

So go and weep if you need to. Mourn the friends you served for a season. Grieve those who won't walk with you into your promise. Allow your sad and lonely days to transform you to become more of who God called you to be.

Embrace your season on the fringe and the outskirts. The Lord is with you, wherever you're planted. Await the preparation. And walk in freedom.

ZIMISM

Strangers
often
disrupt
comfort.

1. Name a friend who was hard for you to lose. Why was it difficult?

2. What is so dangerous about letting your friends define you? What happens when they can't stay?

3. Has God replaced the friends you've lost with new godly ones? If not, why do you think He might be waiting?

4. How can you better weather the storm when your group of friends changes?

6/
TRACKING
TRANSITIONS

I KNEW THAT THE DECISION I WAS about to make would change my life forever. I found myself in St. Louis at a three-day conference, suspended among a sea of thirty thousand worshipers. Everything I had spent countless hours working toward building—a successful company, an abundance of awards, countless hours, and my entire identity—transformed when I did one thing: I obeyed.

In the stands of that stadium, with tears streaming down my face, I listened as a preacher reminded us that while we define success as more money, status, and things, God defines success by sacrifice. We want more riches, fame, and position. God wants obedience. We want to buy more distractions, graduate to nicer surroundings, start new businesses, and own bigger homes. God wants surrender.

I will remember the deeds of the LORD; yes, I will remember your wonders of old.

PSALM 77:11

After the conference, I went back home to Chicago. And it was in this season that I felt the divine providence of God. I didn't know how I would accomplish anything on my own and therefore ended up spending many days in isolation and with only the presence of God. I was broken and weary, but brokenness was the missing ingredient that God needed to do His work best.

The process of selling my company and working alongside the acquiring company for the next eighteen months was a challenging reality. If you're familiar with mergers and acquisitions, it is quite common for the acquiring company to make changes—some drastic and others not so much—to maximize profitability or operational efficiencies.

Because my team had left before the acquisition, I was on my own. I held the responsibility of showing others on this new team

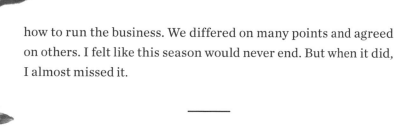

how to run the business. We differed on many points and agreed on others. I felt like this season would never end. But when it did, I almost missed it.

———

Oftentimes we're faced with trying to figure out if we're entering into a new season or if we are still in the midst of a current one. So how can we be sure that the tides are changing and God is bringing us out of one season into a new one?

If we look to nature, we'll find enough parallels and indicators of a changing season. The weather, plant and animal activity, and length of days, among other factors, are strong indicators that a season is changing. In autumn, leaves begin dying and falling to the ground and are often brown in color. The sun sets earlier. The weather cools. In the summer, plants are in full bloom, animal activity is at its peak, and the sun burns brightest. There is an external change happening in the environment that informs us when a new season is coming.

> If we look to nature, we'll find enough parallels and indicators of a changing season.

Changes also happen internally. During the winter many of us suffer from dry skin. We retain less water. Our internal body clocks change.

When I was curious about whether or not a personal season was ending for me, I would track God everywhere I could. I wrote down the dreams and visions that God was giving me and would make note of any circumstantial confirmations. I became relentless, wanting to make sure that in any given season I was able to keep track of what God had done and what He was doing in my life.

Tracking God requires an intimate relationship with Him. While we can't predict what He will do next, we can use what He's already done and what He's revealed to us as a measuring stick for how far along we've come on our journey. I often began by tracking my dreams and then asking questions. *Is God showing me something specific? Were there people in this dream that I recognize? Did something happen to me in that dream?*

Whenever the answers aren't clear to me, I take it to my pastor for deeper revelation. I also make note of answered prayers, a continual process and practice that every Christian should hold dear.

ZIMISM

There is
something great
happening right
now, and I want to
be exactly where
God needs me to
be when it does.

I can't tell you exactly how you will know when your season will end or how a new one will begin; that's God's job. In His sovereignty we can rest in knowing that His timing is perfect. I can, however, share a few things that you can look for.

Sometimes we know that a season has ended because circumstances around us change. We get the job we were praying for. We move to a new city. We get married. We meet new friends after a season of rebuilding. Other times an internal change indicates there is a transition on the horizon. Our perspective shifts. The grace that we once felt is gone. We surrender completely. We disobey God.

When I was let go from the company that had acquired my business, I felt free. I didn't have it all together, but I knew that chapter in my life was closed. Circumstances around me changed. I no longer had to report to work, and I was no longer surrounded by the same colleagues. I was no longer an employee. It was during this season that I wrestled with God the most. Even though I was fearful of who I would become next, I was reminded that in the end I would be made great *with* God.

> Even though I was fearful of who I would become next, I was reminded that in the end, I would be made great *with* God.

A little more than a month later, I was engaged to be married and would soon prepare to become a wife, marking another clear seasonal shift. Your seasons may not be as clearly defined as mine were. They may overlap. You might have a difficult time discerning, and you won't always be able to explain how you know a season is over. It could simply be a feeling. In all things, however, maintaining a posture of prayer and accountability with your spiritual authority is important.

During my senior year in college, I wasn't sure what I wanted to do next. Travel seemed like a helpful option, so I began blindly applying for fellowships all over the world. And I'll never forget the day that I received a letter that would change my life forever.

This letter detailed what my next year would look like. I had just been awarded a fellowship for a full year in any country I chose in Asia. So I did what any normal college graduate would do: I sold everything I owned and moved to India.

As I ended my college season and immediately stepped into another, I had to leave some things behind. The organizations I had started in college would take a backseat while I lived abroad so that I could focus on the present challenges at hand.

In the Bible, Abraham surrendered Isaac when he went up the mountain to sacrifice his son. Rahab surrendered her life when she hid the spies who were sent by God. Moses surrendered his insecurities to lead God's people out of Egypt.

God forbid that we become saddened by the things God requires us to give up. God has so much bigger and better for us than what we've lost—if we only trust Him. In sacrificing the very things that we think we need, we make room for our destiny.

Abraham went from being wealthy to wandering through foreign lands. A vagabond led by a promise—a sharp seasonal shift. King David went from being anointed and chosen by God to lead His people to living on the run. The Bible is teeming with examples of people whose seasons are characterized by internal and external shifts.

> In sacrificing the very things that we think we need, we make room for our destiny.

How can we use tracking as an effective tool for understanding and reflecting on lessons of the season?

Use this seasonal review to track what God is doing and to gain greater clarity on what's happened in your own life, including what you've learned in the process. My hope is that it will prepare and equip you for an even greater season ahead.

STEP 1: GRAPH THE TRUTH

Plot your confirmations and revelations. Some seasons may last for months, while others may span a few years. This exercise will work best if you are able to isolate a specific season, rather than intertwining a few. As a habit, this review will be the most insightful if you are able to write down the things that

God has revealed to you. These may include dreams, answered prayers, encounters with others, visions, circumstances, Scriptures, etc. Take time to list your fears on one side of the page with a corresponding spiritual truth on the other side of the page. For example:

Fears	Scriptural Truths
I'm afraid of losing my job.	I know that God is for me, no matter what happens. • Matthew 6:26 says, "Look at the birds of the air: they neither sow nor reap nor gather into barns, and yet your heavenly Father feeds them. Are you not of more value than they?" • Matthew 6:30 says, "But if God so clothes the grass of the field, which today is alive and tomorrow is thrown into the oven, will he not much more clothe you, O you of little faith?" I know that God will provide for me, even if I never voice it. • Matthew 6:8 says, "Do not be like them, for your Father knows what you need before you ask him."

STEP 2: EXAMINE THE SEASON

Growth

1. What were your two or three biggest lessons of the season?

2. What contributed to them?

3. Which Scripture or Bible passage encouraged you in this season? How?

4. How have you grown over the past twelve months? What's different?

5. What circumstances, people, and desires did you surrender?

6. What skills did you discover during this period?

7. How can you use what you've learned and uncovered for the new season ahead?

8. What was the single largest obstacle you overcame this year? What happened? What has God taught you about it?

9. What were the two or three best decisions you made all year? What did you learn from those experiences?

10. What was the most impactful sermon you've heard regarding your circumstance? What stood out?

Falling Short

1. Where have you disobeyed God? What did you learn from it?

2. What did you hold onto this year that you should have surrendered? What got in the way of letting it go?

3. What were some bad habits you continued or adopted?

4. In what moments have you felt completely hopeless? What did you learn from them?

5. What do you hope God will bless you with in the next season?

6. Where can you extend grace for your shortcomings? Be specific.

Relationships

1. What new relationships enhanced your life and pushed you more toward godliness? Who? How?

2. Has God called you out of any relationships? Who? How?

3. What single person had the biggest impact (positive or negative) on your life? How?

4. Who are your two to three closest relationships? What's one thing you admire about each?

5. Which relationships are you eager to grow?

Themes

1. What were the top lessons that you learned this season?

2. What were the two or three peak moments during this period? What were you doing? What did you learn?

3. What were the two or three lowest moments during this period? What happened? What did you learn?

4. What five to seven words describe this season?

5. What are you most thankful for?

STEP 3: ASSESS YOUR LIFE RIGHT NOW

During this season, there is an incredible opportunity to grow in the Fruit of the Spirit. Complete this table by coloring or filling in the cells up to and including your chosen value for each item. Where do you find yourself now? Which area could use the most growth?

	1	2	3	4	5	6	7	8	9	10
Love										
Joy										
Peace										
Kindness										
Faithfulness										
Gentleness										
Self-Control										
Patience										
Goodness										

STEP 4: PLAN FOR THE NEW SEASON

Growing Forward

1. What three dreams do you desire to see fulfilled in this next season? What's important about them?

2. How can you best acknowledge God's timing? What does that look like tangibly?

3. Which of the nine attributes of the Fruit of the Spirit do you want to develop in this new season?

4. How do you intend to be different by the end of your next season?

5. Who do you believe God wants you to become?

Surrender

1. What do you want or need to shed?

2. What relationships no longer serve you?

3. What questions, burdens, or concerns do you want to bring up to God?

4. How has fear hindered your faith in God?

5. Name a character in the Bible who struggled with his or her faith and ultimately surrendered. What can you learn from that character?

Fears and Roadblocks

1. Are there fears in your life that God wants you to confront? How will you do that?

2. What obstacles do you anticipate you will face going into this new season?

Building Relationships

1. Who in your life deserves more attention?

2. Whom do you desire to build a new relationship with?

Plan Forward

1. What is your Scripture for your new season?

2. What biblical resources do you need to begin to move forward?

3. Whom will you seek help from?

4. How will you structure your prayer life? How will you deepen your fasting life?

5. How can you appreciate and celebrate small wins in your next season?

7

WHEN CRISIS COMES KNOCKING

THE SUN PEERED BETWEEN THE TREES and slowly emerged from behind the mountains. It was a cool, silent morning, and I was alone. The mist, suspended over the open valley below, was a nagging reminder of the weighty burden I carried. While the setting was idyllic, I was in deep turmoil. No amount of time in the wilderness seemed to help. I ran to the farthest corners of the earth to run away from life as I knew it—again. Even as grief enveloped me within the walls of a small, twelfth-century monastery in Umbria, Italy, a cold stone bench near my room's window became my refuge. Umbria, centrally located along Tuscany's border, was where I folded open the pages of the Bible, rummaging for comfort between the lines, begging for God to meet me in the middle of my mess. I rose early every morning in search of hope. I slept when my thoughts overwhelmed me.

> Many are the afflictions of the righteous, but the LORD delivers him out of them all.
>
> PSALM 34:19

A few days earlier, I had boarded a one-way flight to Rome in the hopes of escaping my new reality. And just before that? I made a decision that would change the trajectory of my life forever, and everything that I had worked toward building had suddenly shifted when crisis came knocking.

I had grown comfortable in my role as the founder of a fast-growing travel startup. We were the darlings of the travel industry, having built an unconventional movement by focusing on an unsuspecting audience: Black travelers.

But over the course of one summer, my life grew more and more unrecognizable. My then-boyfriend (now my husband) and I had taken a seven-week break to consecrate ourselves to the Lord. I experienced one of the worst business launches in the history of my company. And eventually I stopped leaving my apartment.

It all culminated in a bold decision—a ball that God threw in my court. It was time to let my company go. I spent hours with my pastors trying to make sense of what was happening. I had wildly vivid dreams. Yet everything in my life that could break began to crumble as I experienced spiritual formation.

When God brought me to this inflection point, I didn't know how much my destiny would depend on my next critical decision. And let me just say, I've been crippled by decision-making throughout my life. In fact, if I could ban it into the galaxy somewhere, and my only decision would be whether I wanted milk in my tea or not, I would. I would rather not make any decision at all, let alone a tough one.

But when a crisis came knocking, I had a decision to make. It was time to trust God and lean in to the spiritual formation. And so I left home to spend time in a monastery, allowing myself to be broken open.

> When God brought me to this inflection point, I didn't know how much my destiny would depend on my next critical decision.

WHEN GOD WANTS MORE

Have you ever considered that God wants more for you than you want for yourself?

I want to introduce you to a woman named Abigail. By all modern standards, Abigail was successful. Her husband Nabal was a wealthy sheepherder in Judah, housing thousands of sheep and goats. One could assume that aside from the fact that Nabal was a particularly rude man, Abigail lived a comfortable life. It may even have been a life that many other wives throughout the region would have pictured as the epitome of success—at least from the outside looking in.

David, born a shepherd and anointed to be the future king of Israel, had been on the run from King Saul with a vagabond crew. When David found out that Nabal had sheared his own sheep, he sent ten of his young men to ask for a gift to not only mark the occasion of the time but also because David's presence in the area meant that Nabal's flocks were protected.

However, instead of offering a grateful welcome, Nabal flung insult after insult at them—an offense so great that David decided to repay it with blood. When Abigail discovered David's plan for her husband, she quietly sent ahead food and drinks, effectively thwarting a potential massacre. When it came time to act, Abigail didn't bury her identity in the life she lived; she nailed it to the promise of a greater future.

> When crisis comes knocking, we have two options: we can either shrink in fear, afraid that we'll lose, or we can make the crucial decision that will propel us into the future.

When crisis comes knocking, we have two options: we can either shrink in fear, afraid that we'll lose, or we can make

the crucial decision that will propel us into the future. Making a decision during a time of deep turmoil or grief can feel excruciating. On top of learning to function in the midst of a challenging time, making a life-altering decision adds to the pressure. *Should I stay? Should I leave? Should I hold on? Should I let go?*

Abigail made a decision. She chose her future. When her husband died roughly ten days later, she went from living a financially comfortable life to one on the run as David's new bride. I wonder what would have happened if she chose to stay.

Like Abigail, we can do powerful things in Christ when we take on His identity at the crossroad. As difficult as it may be, we can always trust that His plans are greater than our crises. Why? When a crisis comes, it can rob us of our joy, our plans, and we often think that it can rob us of our future. But I've got good news: God says that our future is secure in Him.

Maybe you've lost your job or know you need to leave one. Maybe you received a bleak diagnosis. Perhaps you've been betrayed by friends. Or maybe you're experiencing a deep divide within your family.

Has a crisis taken your life on an unexpected turn? Did your comfortable path turn into something unrecognizable? Are you struggling to see how God could allow this to happen to you?

Because He is an omniscient God, His version of better is superior to ours. He sees

ZIMISM

Success by our
standards rarely
aligns with
God's measure
of success.

the bigger picture and the complete plan. He holds our todays and tomorrows in the palm of his hand, constantly guiding us toward truth. I may be limited in how I perceive the world, but God isn't. When we truly rest in His sovereignty, we allow the indecision of the crossroad to melt away.

We can do powerful things in Christ when we take on His identity in the middle of a crisis. The comfort we seek is found once we acknowledge that the same God who brought us to this very moment will equip us with the boldness to make it to the other side.

QUESTIONS FOR REFLECTION

1. When was the last time you were confronted with a crisis?

2. What was your gut reaction to this new turning point? What decision did you make? What happened next?

3. How did God meet you at this particular crossroad?

8/

PACK
LIGHT

MY CHEST CONSTRICTED with a seemingly never-ending grip. My brand-new husband and I had just been driven through the winding, rural roads of Sri Lanka. As scenic as it was nauseating, our five-hour journey from the beach to the tea farms of Uva was otherwise uneventful.

On that journey, however, I lived somewhere between panic attack and Scriptural meditation. The truth is—it wasn't easy to feel holy when everything was collapsing around me.

Our home for the next few days would be a beautiful, colonial seventeenth-century Georgian-style bungalow, once owned by a Scottish tea planter. I took a deep breath, yawning in part because my body was tired, but also because my brain was sending a "need more oxygen" signal to my lungs.

"I am the true vine, and my Father is the vinedresser. Every branch in me that does not bear fruit he takes away, and every branch that does bear fruit he prunes, that it may bear more fruit."

JOHN 15:1-2

Surrounded by twelve hundred acres of tea plantations, we were hours away from help if we needed it. Although I had been here before—and there's often a strange sense of security in the familiar—I was suddenly aware that we were thousands of miles away from home if a sudden disaster called for a medivac, or worse.

God, You're faithful. You care for me. You won't let anything happen to me.

My thoughts raced from panic to prayer. With every strained breath I thought that the day would be my last, and my adventurous eight-week honeymoon to celebrate our month-old marriage would suddenly come to an end.

I felt lightheaded. It was difficult to stand.

I found temporary comfort on my husband's chest as tears trickled down my face. A song declaring God's faithfulness streamed through my laptop speakers and rested on my heart. I wept.

If ever I had been scared, it was always the fear of dying in an unknown land, far away from those I loved and that which I knew. This was it.

The threat felt real. I couldn't go out like this. I called my mom, who reassured me that it was nothing more than an altitude adjustment. After all, we did just travel from sea level to upward of six thousand feet in just a few hours.

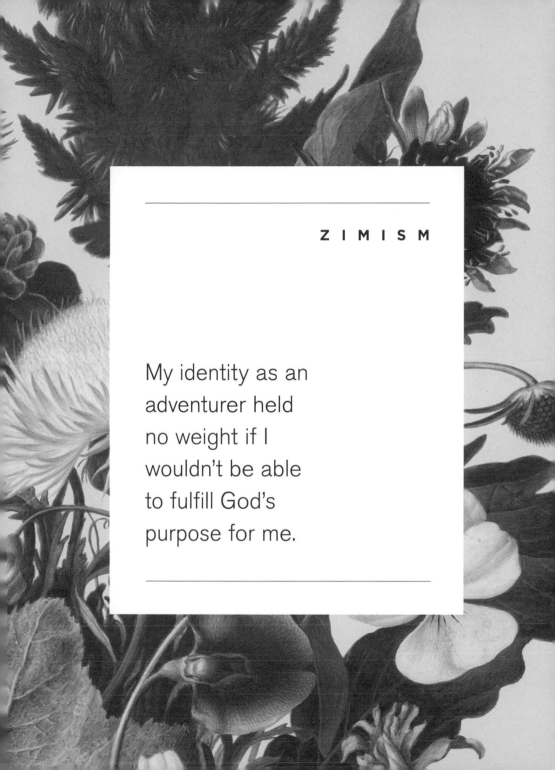

ZIMISM

My identity as an
adventurer held
no weight if I
wouldn't be able
to fulfill God's
purpose for me.

During dinner, instead of focusing on my husband or the mezze platter of home-cooked food, I was busy, albeit discreetly, searching the Internet for symptoms of altitude sickness. I called the waiter over and explained my symptoms, but the language barrier prevented the beat of my fear from connecting.

He offered me a simple Ayurvedic concoction in tea form: ginger, black pepper, and other herbs and spices. I instantly felt better. My nerves began to simmer. My countenance lightened, and I regained confidence in my conversation.

Later in the evening, as we sat by the fireplace, a nagging ache began to cloud my heart: the myriad of Internet searches, the conversations with my mother, and a well-known Sri Lankan Ayurvedic tea provided me with more relief than meditating on the promises of God. A quick call home or the harmless medication wasn't an issue in and of itself, but I propped them up on the pedestal of my heart. I had gone first to the thing—anything—that I thought could provide the quickest relief and missed out on an opportunity to strengthen my faith.

So often we weigh the habits of our past against the sovereignty of God. Our identity tells us that what we're familiar with is the

ZIMISM

Elevation requires
us to burn off
the things that
weigh us down.

comfort that we need. It tricks us into believing that our coping mechanisms should remain in the seen versus the unseen.

But what happens when we truly take God at His Word? When we know without question that His promises are just as tangible and real as the temporary solutions we seek? What I learned in that moment, as the fire warmed my flustered face, was the same thing that God tried to teach me years before: some people try to bring something, but nothing is what's best.

We try to bring the people, circumstances, and mindsets of our past into our future. We want the common comforts of those friends or those circumstances. But when God wants to elevate us, something's gotta give. Just as a car drives forward, it burns fuel. As a plane takes off, it releases fuel.

Sometimes people, patterns of thinking, and habits have no place in where God is taking you. I learned that the mindset of my past wouldn't work for my future understanding. God wants us to be more fruitful, more productive, and more like Him so that we can be more effective for His Kingdom. And to be effective for the Kingdom, we not only have to shed the identities we've worked so hard to build, we must then affix ourselves to the One who matters. We have to be pruned. Pruning is the careful removal of living, dying, or dead plant parts. Why do plants need to be pruned often? To make way for better growth—and a heartier bloom.

MAINTAINING PLANT HEALTH

Gardeners spend hours pruning their plants to protect them from pests and diseases that can enter from dead or dying wood and broken branches. For a moment, imagine that you are a bush. You have an acre full of neighbors beside you that provide nests, food, and foliage for nearby wildlife. Every so often, your gardener's job is to meet you with a sharp shear and remove anything that is causing you harm—whether you are aware of it or not. The gardener cuts these pieces away, knowing that diseases and pests can stunt your growth as they feed off the nutrients that you provide. If left unkept, you could end up as a dry shell of your former glory.

How much greater of a gardener is God? He sees the things that hold us back that are often hiding in our blind spots—right where we don't see them—and swiftly cuts them off to make sure that our growth isn't restricted.

That hustle mentality that I picked up as an entrepreneur? Snipped away to make space for the restful Sabbath I needed for the next season. Those friends who cause us to stumble? Cut off to make way for new, godly ones. That destructive social habit that we developed just to keep up with the crowd? Gone so that we can establish healthy boundaries, in real life.

TRAINING A PLANT

Plant training involves controlling the growth of a plant by manipulating its direction, shape, or size, with the ultimate goal of improving its appearance; increasing fruit size, quality, and yield; protecting it from damage; and keeping it from danger. Sometimes this process involves attaching the plant to a solid structure, like a wall, fence, or post, depending on the plant and the desired outcome.

When I was younger, I used to get in trouble—a lot. *Mischief* could have been my middle name. I stole things when I was a teenager. I was involved with the wrong crowd of friends. I would sneak out of the house in the middle of the night. Truth was rarely on my lips. I desperately wanted to fit in and didn't want anyone telling me what to do. But as I grew older, the only discipline necessary for the crime at hand often ended with my mom in tears. There was no grandstanding. The pain of what I had done over the years had gone from a loud voice and spankings to a quiet whimper.

Mischief could have been my middle name.

In a desperate measure, my mom enrolled me into a magnet school—full of the weirdest kids I had ever met. The friends who influenced me to lie, cheat, and steal in order to be cool and to fit in were eventually replaced with new ones who gave me permission to be my unique, quirky, and very uncool self—revealing part of my identity to me.

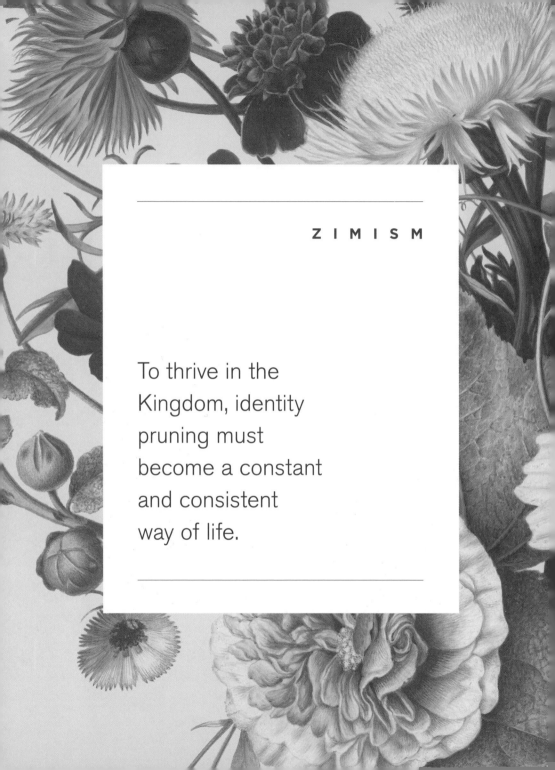

ZIMISM

To thrive in the
Kingdom, identity
pruning must
become a constant
and consistent
way of life.

I realized as I grew older that the spankings, the new school, the hard conversations, and the tears all served as a training ground for who I would become. I learned the hard way that parents discipline those they love. Since we are God's prized possessions, made in His precious image, His love requires discipline.

Like plants, in order to produce the best fruit and the highest yield, we need to be paired with a solid structure. Hebrews 12:11 teaches us, "For the moment all discipline seems painful rather than pleasant, but later it yields the peaceful fruit of righteousness to those who have been trained by it." In my case, I needed to become firmly rooted in God.

ZIMISM

We can't
confuse our
flaws with
having high
standards.

IMPROVING THE QUALITY OF LEAVES

During premarital counseling, my fiancé shared with our pastor that one of the traits that he least appreciated about me was my pickiness.

Ouch.

You mean my weird relationship with dirty tile grout is a problem? That if it exists anywhere in a hotel, we can't stay?

Yes. Things just like that.

I had to learn that my pickiness was useful in certain situations—like finding godly friends and a godly partner—but much *less* useful in other areas—like wanting every piece of furniture to align perfectly with my invisible vision board at home.

Fun fact: I made my husband give away most of his furniture because it didn't fit the aesthetic.

When we trust and obey God, watered and nurtured by His Word, we become transformed more and unto His likeness. This process is called *sanctification,* and it is the intended result of salvation for every man and woman. The traits that God has given us are His to enhance. Even our flaws are His to transform. Imagine having your greatest weakness turned into a testimony of God's grace. As we navigate new seasons and learn to leave what's behind us, we should honor who we are, but not hold on to the traits that need to go.

MANAGING GROWTH

Every gardener wants a beautiful harvest.

In a similar way, God desires for us to become more fruitful, more productive, and more like Him so that we can be more effective for His Kingdom. This means we need to be pruned. We have to be trained. Our growth demands it. Pruning may be one of the most painful things we will experience. But without it, we'll never reach our full purpose, destiny, our mission, our calling, and we won't be able to understand our true identity.

God even trims branches that already bear fruit so that they may be even *more* fruitful. God wants us to live—not just *any* life but an extremely *abundant* one! As we transition into new seasons, we often try to bring old relationships, friendships, careers, patterns of thinking, and habits from our past into our future, primarily because it's what we're used to. But if life has taught me anything, it's that bringing nothing is best.

> If life has taught me anything, bringing nothing is best.

Following God wholeheartedly means that we are constantly looking forward with our eyes fixed on Christ. In the early days of farming, if someone wanted to plow a straight line, they would have to affix their eyes to an object in the distance. But if they constantly looked back to check their progress, they might veer over to the one side, ruining any progress that was made.

Constantly looking back at the lives we've left behind steals our present and robs us of our future. When we learn to follow, submit, and keep our eyes on God, we recognize that He alone will make our paths straight.

QUESTIONS FOR REFLECTION

1. What habits, people, and mindsets are you bringing from your past into your future?

2. What in your life needs to be pruned?

3. What does "packing light" mean to you as you move into this new season?

4. Recall a previous time when your life hit an inflection point. How did letting go of old mindsets or old relationships help you navigate your new beginning?

9

WE DON'T NEED RAIN

WE HAD SPENT A SUNNY FEW DAYS in Tel Aviv, a city on Israel's Mediterranean coast.

"You all brought amazing weather. Normally around this time it's nonstop rain," a friend shared.

It was Christmas Eve, and we were due to head up north to the Sea of Galilee. We lingered for a few more hours than we had originally intended so that we could soak in the sun. As we packed everything into the rental car and set out for our drive, we felt an ache in our hearts.

We drove up Highway 6, one of the main interstate highways in Israel. The night felt cool, and if we'd had the chance to stop, we could have looked up and witnessed a kaleidoscope of stars. I glanced at the weather app on my phone and sighed. One-hundred percent chance of rain for the next week. That meant that all of the sites we wanted to see—Capernaum, where Jesus started His ministry; Bethsaida and Chorazin, cities once cursed by Jesus that now lay barren; and so many others— would now be visited in the pouring rain, during the week of Christmas no less.

> Sow for yourselves righteousness; reap steadfast love; break up your fallow ground, for it is the time to seek the LORD, that he may come and rain righteousness upon you.
>
> **HOSEA 10:12**

I had waited for months to visit these sites again and had hoped that they would be just as beautiful as they were when I first visited. Now we would have to deal with low visibility, wet clothes, and soggy, muddy shoes. We would try to make the best of it, but it just wasn't quite the experience that we were hoping for.

Rain has evolved into what some would consider a modern-day nuisance, where it once was the lifeblood of our communities. Before irrigation systems, watersheds, and other mechanisms used to store water, rain was essential to fuel crop growth.

No rain? No food. A famine could, in essence, wipe out an entire community. I considered the paradoxical nature of it all.

What farmers required, we dismissed. What they needed for growth, we avoided. When we shun the rain, we stunt our development. It's essentially spiritual deferment.

Fallow ground refers to uncultivated, unsown, and inactive ground. It is often uncultivated for a few seasons to restore its fertility. If rain falls on fallow ground, nothing happens. When the ground hasn't been tilled, there can be no harvest. Fallow ground needs to be broken up to prepare it for growth.

By now, we know that all growth comes from rain. But when we don't surrender our outcomes to God, we get the unappealing substitute for growth instead of the real thing.

PHANTOM GROWTH VS. THE REAL THING

There is no substitute for real growth. With plants, sometimes a vine can grow and grow, appearing healthy, and not produce any blossoms or fruit. We can do all of the "right things" while still holding onto things that stunt our spiritual growth—like the romantic relationship that we hold onto even though we know that he is not God's best for us; or the slightly toxic circle of friends who once helped us grow but now hold us back; or even the job that pays well but is in direct conflict with our purpose.

There is no substitute for real growth.

The real thing looks more like a temporary brokenness that comes with moving on from an empty relationship and the new fulfillment we find in connection with Christ. Real growth is found in the godly friends who don't allow you to avoid the difficult spiritual lessons and who support us along the way. It's found in a job that nurtures our God-given gifts and allows our testimony to reach and touch those around us.

We often want the Lord to bless what we haven't submitted to Him. To truly understand the importance of spiritual rain in our lives, we need to understand the concept of breaking up fallow ground. Even though we all desire growth, we cheat ourselves by failing to prepare our hearts, minds, and other areas of our lives to be transformed.

DESERT SEASONS

A few years ago, while traveling through Cambodia by motorcycle, I noticed how important a single commodity was in the lives of all whom I came across: water.

Throughout the Bible water flows through the pages of Scripture. God's Word is full of passages that link water to God's creating, blessing, and saving work. While the Israelites wandered through the desert, they forgot their identity. They forgot that they were God's chosen people.

God often brings us into desert seasons not to harm us but to prepare us. He will reposition or remove the things that we turn to when we are tempted to fill a void. And He'll use that season, while painful, to break, reassemble, and strengthen us. It's His divine preparation.

There are lessons that we can learn only when we're walking in a dry place. When our friends have turned their backs on us. When our job lets us go. When that sickness makes its way back. When we feel like God isn't listening.

> There are lessons that we can learn only when we're walking in a dry place.

Moses told the people that not only was God about to release the fullness of the promise into their lives—the Promised Land full of milk and honey—but He had prepared their hearts to live large in the abundance of His provision. Imagine getting the very thing we wanted before the preparation. Would we not corrupt it?

We are always either walking toward a desert season, currently wandering through one, or walking out of the wilderness. As long as we follow God's leading, we will never thirst. The longer we try to do things our way, the longer we will thirst after the things that can't fully quench us.

People are taught that if they ever find themselves lost in the wild, they are to look for signs of life.

Life happens near water. Plants are born. Food grows. Goods are transported.

Before pipes carried water around the city, towns congregated near water. People would come and collect water and transport it back to their homes. Land along rivers was fertile. If the land was fertile, crops could grow. If crops could grow, then people could be fed. It was in the valley that people were able to get their most precious life-sustaining resource: water.

When I think about the times that I've been in a literal valley—unable to see the mountaintop—it's what I did in the valley that gave me the strength to make it to the summit.

I filled up on flowing water. I gathered the food that grew close to the riverbank. I allowed myself to be nourished by the river, spending days there preparing for the journey ahead.

The Bible tells us in John 7:38 that those who believe in Jesus shall have rivers of living water flow from within them.

During some of the lowest points of my life, camping out at the river is what gave me strength for the climb. When I was weak, water replenished. When I was tired, water refreshed. When I was hot, water tempered.

What I've learned over the years is that God is the only One who can quench my inner thirst, the thirst of my soul. When I thought people, success, money, or fame could satisfy, it was only through God that I was made full and He began to flow out of me. When I started studying His Word on my own, separating myself from this world and unto Him, the desires of the world fell out of focus.

> I can get everything I need at the river.

I can get everything I need at the river. I gather instruction. I can talk to the locals about the safest routes to the top. And because I'm so full on the nutrients and instruction that I gathered in the valley, I have the strength and wisdom to climb to the top of the mountain. I'm able to pour out unto

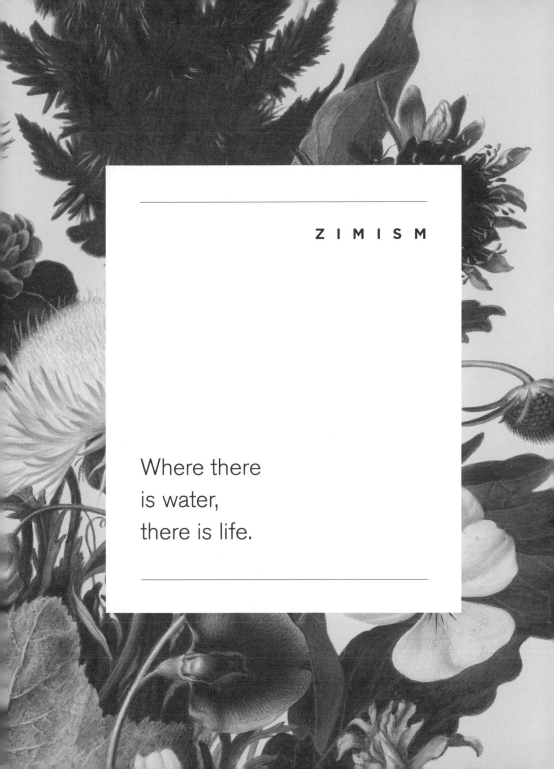

ZIMISM

Where there
is water,
there is life.

any others that pass by as I make my way up. I can pour out what I've gathered in the valley.

During our lowest moments in the valley, we must stay close to the river. During the rise to the top, we must stay grounded and remember the wisdom we gathered in the valley. And when we finally come to the clearing at the top of the mountain, we'll be able to see all that the Lord brought us from and the newness that He's bringing us into.

It's important to note that water can often come from unlikely sources. In Isaiah 48:21 we're told that water flowed from a rock. *A rock!*

Now, I don't know about you, but I didn't grow up knowing there were reservoirs of water hidden inside of rocks. Since we know that water represents life and we can't survive without it, this should come as no surprise: God keeps new life hidden in those hard places.

That boyfriend who dumped you. Those friends who left you. The job that let you go. All of the things that you think are going wrong—God will break it wide open so that His Truth can flow freely. That water will wash you, invigorate, and carry you.

———

As we approached the final stretch of our Cambodian motorcycle adventure, it began to rain. And not just any rain but a torrential downpour. It was one of the most surreal experiences I've ever witnessed. For me, it symbolized a purification. And it signified a lesson that I would later learn: purpose will come from the moment the rock splits.

I desperately wanted sun in Israel. A bit shallow for some, I'm sure, but it was important for me to experience the Sea of Galilee the way that Jesus had. However, I realized that maybe this was the way that He had also experienced it: cold and rainy some days, hot and dry on others.

Yielding my expectations for perfect weather was simply another example of giving up my desire to control aspects of my life that God desperately needed to change. It was always difficult for me to let go of circumstances, because I always had a perfect outcome in mind. But the only way for me to get the real thing was to break up the fallow ground of my own expectations to prepare for a season of harvest.

> The only way for me to get the real thing was to break up the fallow ground of my own expectations to prepare for a season of harvest.

Once I let God into each area of my life, piece by piece, things started to transform. My relationship blossomed into a healthy marriage, my industry friends were replaced with godly ones, and my career shifted right before my eyes.

When I decided to give my ears to Christ—listening to Christian music only—it unlocked a new world of intimacy with Him. I knew that what I watched or listened to would show up in my lifestyle; this simple decision removed me from lyrics that were displeasing to God. The things that we allow to occupy our minds always determine our speech or actions. The Bible tells us to think about what is true, noble, right, pure, lovely, and admirable.

When I look back at the years where I experienced the most growth, I am in awe of God's providence. I hadn't gone through a good storm in years and—oh my—the downpour brought tremendous growth. In the thick of the storm, I cried often, feeling tormented and crushed in spirit. As difficult as it was, I again begged God to hold me there as long as He needed to use me. And again He honored that faithfulness.

While our wounds may not be our fault, our healing is our responsibility. We can stay down, or we can get up. It's our choice. God will never waste pain. In fact, His plan is to grow beauty and purpose out of it. I had to remember that ministry was being birthed from my misery.

The Bible, which is complete, inerrant, living, and active, is God's provision for us to know Him, serve Him, and grow in relationship with Him. It shows us where we lack. The Word of God proves us in need of a Savior. So long as our hearts are prepared and the fallow ground is broken up and ready for rain, God will provide the increase.

ZIMISM

I broke the fallow
ground of what I
listened to, and
God released the
rain. And when it
rained, it poured.

QUESTIONS FOR REFLECTION

1. What are areas of your life that need to be surrendered back to God?

2. What are you afraid will happen if you completely surrender this area to God? Be specific.

3. Name a time in your life when you completely surrendered your will to God. What happened next?

4. In what ways has God brought beauty and growth out of a painful time in your life?

5. What are some unlikely sources from which God has poured out on you His life-giving water?

10 /

THE SHADOW
PROVES THE
SUNSHINE

ON THE SAME DAY THAT I WAS LAID OFF from the company I started, I, along with forty other strangers, drove up the coast to Zikhron Ya'Akov, one of the oldest towns in the modern history of Israel. I had sensed that this day was coming for a long time.

Seven months earlier, I received a call from a work colleague whom I had never met personally but who informed me that the executive team was planning on firing me once the time was right. The weightiness of his words jolted my spirit. Cracks began to form on the surface of my heart. I started to prepare myself spiritually, emotionally, and financially. Shortly thereafter, I applied for a ten-day immersion experience in Israel. Never having been, I was intrigued by the opportunity to experience Jewish culture firsthand.

> Arise, shine,
> for your light
> has come,
> and the glory
> of the LORD has
> risen upon you.
>
> ISAIAH 60:1

But for the seven months leading up to the trip, there was a sultry cloud that hung over my head. Not knowing when I would be fired from my job meant that I often teetered on the edge of security and peril. I felt disposable. I was repeatedly discouraged. I didn't feel like I mattered. And while I couldn't sense the sunshine, I eventually learned that the shadow proved its very existence.

In the depths of my own shame, God was teaching me that a casted shadow proved His presence. Who was I that God was so mindful of me? He masterfully planned my last day at my job to coincide in a land all His own. I had been blooming all along—but the shadow of shame kept me from recognizing God's providence and protection.

Even in the shadow, we're still under the protection of God. Blooming is simply a shift from shadow to sunshine. It's the final stage of growth before the cycle begins again. Although blooming isn't meant to last forever, we can find hope in the order of nature.

The seasons that I had spent tilling the ground of my heart, uprooting mindsets that failed to serve God, and planting the seeds of humility were honored in the sunshine. The pain of sacrifice was tempered by the warmth of the sun.

Just as the pollen and nectar from flowers nourish entire ecosystems, with God we will encourage and strengthen others. We will operate in our purpose—one that we've uncovered in our secret place with Jesus.

We learn to understand the guarantee of fresh oil, a process through which we become more like Christ. We begin to recognize the importance of both the pause and the praise, and the tension of its duality. When they can't stay, God clears the path for more fruitful relationships.

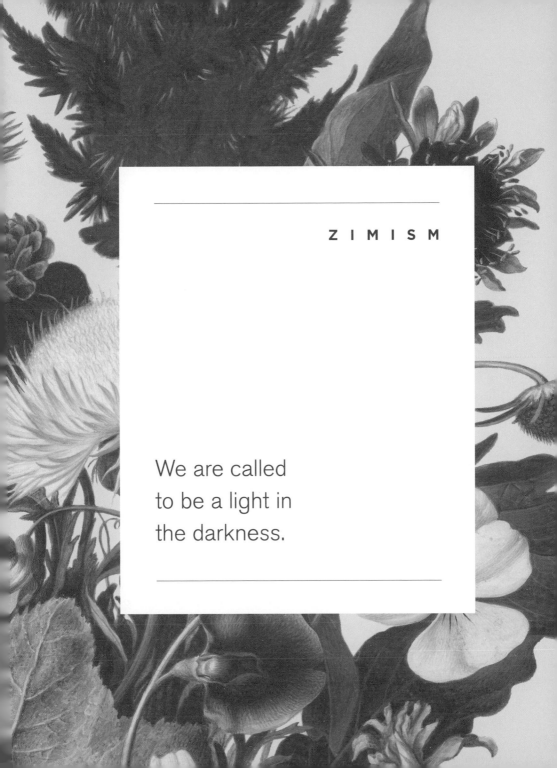

ZIMISM

We are called
to be a light in
the darkness.

The last day with my company carried with it a deep peace. My experience in Israel was just beginning. In fact, I wrote a chapter of this book in Jerusalem. Revelation after revelation began to flow like cascading rivers. Life accelerated after that day. The tension of the months to follow reminded me that the pain of my past would never outweigh the promises of the future.

I've learned that life parallels nature in undeniable ways. By the time a flower blooms, so much has already happened behind the scenes. Plants have an internal clock powered by photoreceptors that help them sense when sunlight increases and days become longer. When it's time to bloom, a plant begins to produce a protein in its leaves that travels to the tips of shoots, undergoing molecular transformations that form flowers.

> I've learned that life parallels nature in undeniable ways.

On November 4, 2019, the flowers of my new season began to blossom. God blessed me with a companion for life. Forged together by the grace of His providence, I felt the sunshine yet again. It was time to bloom. And this time I understood the purpose of the shadow.

Daring to bloom takes courage—not only to celebrate the harvest but to be humble enough to honor the cycle. Now is the time to stand in the sunshine—for although temporary, it is proof of the promises of God.

And if you haven't seen a bloom quite yet, hold on. It's coming.

Father, we humbly come before You, thanking You for not only what You've done but for who You are.

Lord, I thank You for the life that You've given me, and although I may not always love what happens in this life, I know that You love me deeply. Please forgive me for the ways that I may have led people away from You, both knowingly and unknowingly. I thank You for the promise of a renewed and transformed mind.

I need Your help surrendering areas of my life to You. I know that if You are in the midst, all things are good. Help me to understand that living for You brings joy, hope, and peace. And the transformations that You want to bless me with can only happen when I step out of my will and into Your Will.

Lord, I thank You for your continued grace and mercy during this process. I thank You for the reminder that my fallow ground, once broken up, will provide a bountiful harvest.

I thank You that I belong to You and that Your love lives through me.

In Jesus' name I pray, amen.

ACKNOWLEDGMENTS

I BEGAN WRITING THIS BOOK well before I had a book deal. A few years ago, I sat along a quiet beach outside of Barcelona, mulling over the blank digital diary that would become the seedlings of *Dare to Bloom*. To say that this hasn't been a challenging undertaking would be telling a half truth and a full lie. Poring over every word, I've struggled with the intent of each sentence and the impact of each paragraph. I have mourned my former life and cut open half-healed wounds. While I have many people to thank, none of this would have been possible without my dear husband.

Jason, my life is illuminated by your love. God knew how our story would unfold, yet He laced it with only the things that would grow us—heartbreak, sacrifice, consecration, and deep selfless love. Some days, I find myself stealing an extra gaze while you sleep. I wake up each day indebted to a God who so perfectly created the one whom my soul loves. I can't wait to grow old together. To love our children well. To travel deeply. You have my heart forever. I love you endlessly.

To my friends-turned-family—Chadricks, Isaiah, Ngozi, Angie, Warren, Anwar, Chris, Bruce, Danielle, and Nazneen—thank you for standing with me, season after season and year after year.

To my brothers and sisters—Chebem, Nkechi, Jaron, Ugonna, and Nnenna—thank you for riding the waves of life with me, no matter how far we find ourselves from each other. Sylvanus and Chebem, we're in it 'til the wheels fall off. Thanks for being there since the beginning.

To my mom, your fierce love has protected me since the minute I was born. Thank you for nurturing my eccentricities and telling me the truth, even when it hurts. To Charlie, thank you for loving my mom well. You are a force all your own. To my father, thank you for your courage to begin again.

To Bishop and Vicki Gonzalez, and Pastor Rick and Angela Gonzalez, you have kept me spiritually sharp since the day my broken heart stepped through your church doors. Thank you for the endless podcast revisions, the extra set of eyes, the prayers, the guidance, the correction, the fellowship, and the deep conversations. I pray that everyone can experience spiritual authority in the ways that I have in this lifetime. Thank you for living the Acts 2 message and for being a Holy Ghost–filled church. To my ICF family, thank you for being an endless source of love and inspiration.

My first company was full of passion and rife with mistakes. In the four short years that I owned Travel Noire, I learned the tension of true leadership. Many days I failed. But today I stand more conscious and even more humble. To the original Travel Noire team—Gaston, Moraa, Shedisha, Bunge, Maya, Skye, and Leandra—I think about our glory days often. Thank you for your sacrifice and your service. Thank you for showing me what the mark of real leadership looks like. To our advisors, who were with us through it all—Stephen, Courtney, Alicin, and Andrea—thank you for believing in me. To our TN Experiences partners, experience designers, and photographers in South Africa, Brazil, Italy, Morocco, Indonesia, Cuba, and Tanzania, thank you for trusting us with your talent and for teaching me how transformative good leadership really is.

My world of travel began with the Luce Scholars program. Thank you, Ling, Michelle, David, and Mandakini, for turning a little naive girl into a global citizen. I'm confident that Travel Noire would not exist without this program and your ironclad dedication to it. Thank you, Nick and Kerry, for taking me into your home and sharing with me your countless adventure stories. Kerry, we'll miss you forever. Rest in peace. Thank you, Mackenzie, for braving India with me. To the entire 2011–2012 class, #LuceLove.

To my alma mater, UNCG, you taught me the power of being a big fish in a small pond. The support that I received equipped me to think both critically and independently. It is here where I cloned my first gene. It's where I won my first national awards. It's where I learned how to organize communities. My work with Ignite Greensboro and the International Civil Rights Museum fueled my love for building community. Dr. LaJeunesse, the years I spent in your lab taught me the power of devotion to cause. Thank you for being a selfless scientist. Thank you, Debbie, David, Chris, and the entire 2011 University Relations team, for believing in me and amplifying my voice. Thank you, Adrienne, for the life lessons, then and now.

Thank you to my HarperCollins family for championing my story. Danielle, your email found me on a day I desperately needed a sign from God. Bonnie, thank you for partnering with me to refine my words. Thank you, Tiffany, for designing a cover that spoke to this message. To the entire HCCP team, I can't wait for what's next.

Lisa, my powerhouse agent. Thank you for taking the meeting in the last inning and for believing in my ability to tell unconventional stories for people of faith. You stopped taking on new authors but found it in your heart to accept one more. Thank you.

To those who have taught me the most difficult lessons—in friendships, in business, in love, and in loss—thank you. To the ones I've gained and to those I've lost, thank you for pushing me closer to who God called me to be.

Jesus, thank You for this honor. I will do my best. Keep me.

IMAGE CREDITS

All images courtesy of Zim Flores.

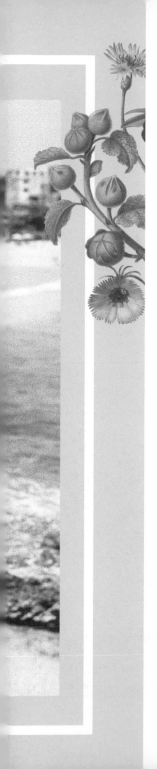

ABOUT THE AUTHOR

NAMED A LEADER USING HER VOICE and talent to elevate humanity by Oprah Winfrey, Zim Flores (née Ugochukwu) is the founder of Italicist, an online styling service that helps women discover modest clothing they love, without the time commitment. Previously she was the CEO of Travel Noire, a boutique travel company reaching millions of travelers each month. In 2017 she sold the company to pursue Christ. A serial entrepreneur, Zim is a Forbes "30 Under 30" awardee who has been featured in *The New York Times*, *TIME*, *ELLE*, *Glamour Magazine*, *The Nation*, *Essence*, and NPR, among others. She often writes in faraway places and lives with her husband in Illinois. Connect with her at www.zimism.com and @zimism.